The idea of whole-life discipleship could hardly be more important. This stimulating book is both thoughtful and immensely practical. I highly recommend it to anyone with a leadership role.
Stephen Gaukroger, Clarion Trust

Beautifully engaging, elegantly simple, gloriously practical. This isn't a seven-step programme, but a traveller's guide for a great journey – the transformation of church culture to whole-life disciple-making. I hope and pray many will use it.
James Lawrence, CPAS

From churches involved in the Imagine Project

Neil's book reminds every believer about the necessary mindset we must maintain of being 'On Errand for Jesus!' 24/7. Having the faculty at LICC take us through the Imagine Project teaching series in our local church was a breakthrough point for us, and we wished the series would never end. Now that we have Neil's book, the series doesn't have to end! We have in our hands a fantastic guide to how we can further unpack perhaps the most important challenge facing the twenty-first-century church: that of whole-life discipleship. Thanks, Neil.
Rev. 'Biyi Ajala, Pastor, Holding Forth the Word Ministry, Milton Keynes, UK

Reading Neil Hudson's book as the leader of one of the pilot churches described in the book, at a distance of two or three years, is a salutary experience. The discussions and lessons from the project period have been brought to a focus which sharply reminds this leader of those lessons and how easily they have been forgotten, or only half-remembered. As Neil Hudson writes in the book, changing a culture requires persistent championing, and in the hurly-burly of church life the intention can be too easily lost! Thankfully, he has written his book, and through it we can be reminded of the small but significant changes that we

need to make that will eventually lead to a radically different outcome for our church. The best thing since sliced bread may not be this book – but it's a close call! Read it carefully.
Kim Lau, Pastor of Manchester Chinese Christian Church

Neil writes with clarity and urgency about the need to make whole-life disciples. Yet it's because he goes one step further that you should read this book: *Imagine Church* offers the outlines of a strategy which can be tailored to your own church context, whatever that may be. And since the book is written by a pastor-thinker, who not only understands first-hand the day-to-day challenges of disciple-making, but has also spent a lot of time listening to other pastors, you'll find that Neil's answers are worth exploring.
Chloe Lynch, Leader, LifeGiving Church, London

This book rings true because it beats with the heart of biblical Christianity, recognizing that every aspect of the life of a believer belongs to the Lord. It's a welcome change from a conversation that can too often focus on church programmes, projects, numbers and so on. However, it is much more than that! It reminds us that God is powerfully at work in our world and calls us to cooperate with his Spirit by being prepared to follow him, whatever the circumstances. In this way, Neil Hudson convincingly argues that there are endless possibilities for radical transformation of our wider communities.
John Owen, Academic Registrar, Regents Theological College, Worcestershire; South Manchester Family Church

Imagine Church

Imagine
Church

Releasing
Whole-Life
Disciples

Neil Hudson

Foreword by Graham Cray

INTER-VARSITY PRESS
Norton Street, Nottingham NG7 3HR, England
Email: ivp@ivpbooks.com
Website: www.ivpbooks.com

First published 2012
Reprinted 2013, 2015

British Library Cataloguing in Publication Data
A catalogue record for this book is available from the British Library.

ISBN: 978–1–84474–566–1

Set in Dante 12/15pt
Typeset in Great Britain by CRB Associates, Potterhanworth, Lincolnshire
Printed and bound in Great Britain by Ashford Colour Press Ltd, Gosport,
Hampshire

Inter-Varsity Press publishes Christian books that are true to the Bible and that
communicate the gospel, develop discipleship and strengthen the church for its
mission in the world.

Inter-Varsity Press is closely linked with the Universities and Colleges Christian
Fellowship, a student movement connecting Christian Unions in universities and
colleges throughout Great Britain, and a member movement of the International
Fellowship of Evangelical Students. Website: www.uccf.org.uk

Contents

Acknowledgments

Thanks to the 5,000 . . . and probably more

A quite extraordinary number of people have contributed to the insights and words in this book. Something over 5,000. And that may be modest. We are extremely grateful for all the kindness, generosity, wisdom, hard work and grace that have been so freely extended.

From January 2007, the following churches joined us in the Imagine Pilot Project, exploring over three years how church communities might learn to engage in the central task of whole-life disciple-making:

- Bushey Baptist Church
- Christ Church, Bedford (Anglican)
- Christ Church, Selly Park, Birmingham (Anglican)
- Christ Church, Ewell (Independent)
- City Church, Manchester (Independent)
- Dewsbury Elim Church (Elim Pentecostal)
- Ealing LifeGiving Church (Independent)
- Greenock, East End NCD (Church of Scotland)
- Grimsby Neighbourhood Church (Elim Pentecostal)

- Holding Forth the Word, Milton Keynes (Independent)
- Manchester Chinese Christian Church
  (Non-denominational)
- St Mary Magdalen, Bermondsey (Anglican)
- St Mary Magdalen, Sheet, Hants (Anglican)
- St Ninian's and St Andrew's, Lamesley (Anglican)
- South Manchester Family Church (Newfrontiers)
- The Vine, Cranbrook (Independent)

The opportunity to work with a variety of churches in very different contexts meant that we were able to test out theories, ideas and resources, learn from success and failure, and develop the key lessons and principles that have emerged.

In every case, the pilot churches were really welcoming, committed to the work of disciple-making and willing for an outsider to get close enough to understand the inner dynamics of their church community. The stories that appear here all come from this work. And there were many more, which is a reason to be greatly encouraged. But we couldn't tell them all. We want to thank all those communities for their partnership in this work of the gospel. And we want to pray God's continued blessing on your future.

We want to pay tribute to those who funded the project, to the scores of individuals and to our partners at the Jerusalem Trust, the Alvor Charitable Trust, the Maurice and Hilda Laing Charitable Trust, the Hinchley Charitable Trust and Deo Gloria Trust who not only were willing to release finance to us, but also took a keen interest in all that happened and shared their wisdom with us along the way.

But there were also hundreds of others whose contributions shaped the project before it began – our partners at the Evangelical Alliance who published Mark Greene's original essay, *Imagine: How We Can Reach the UK*, the 800 or so people who completed questionnaires about whole-life discipleship and their church, the hundreds of leaders who came to a series of consultations on the theory and results, the 600 or so leaders who came to six seminars on whole-life disciple-making in the local church enthusiastically run by our partners at RUN (Reaching the Unchurched Network), the many people who contributed to the consultation on disciple-making that led to the book *Let My People Grow*, edited by Tracy Cotterell and Mark Greene.

And then there are 1,200 people who support our work at the London Institute for Contemporary Christianity (LICC) – in faithful prayer, and in sharing wisdom and finance – all in the cause of envisioning and equipping whole-life disciples for fruitful mission out on the frontline. We may never be able to thank you face to face, but you need to know how significant your support has been. To all of you, thank you.

Over the years, we have received invitations to share our passions at various denominational gatherings, which has meant that we have had ongoing conversations that have refocused and refined our thinking. In particular we want to thank Rev. Jonathan Edwards and Rev. Ian Bunce from the Baptist Union; Rev. John Glass and Rev. Nigel Tween from the Elim Pentecostal Church; Rev. Dr Martyn Atkins, Mr John Ellis and Rev. Jenny Ellis from the Methodist Connexion. In addition, Kate Byrom's support from IVP meant that this did see the light of day.

Finally, this has been a work that is possible because of the support of colleagues at LICC. All of them have asked about its progress and prayed for the whole project from the beginning, and for that I am most grateful. But there are a couple who do deserve a special mention. I began working on the Imagine Project with Tracy Cotterell. It was her initial belief that I could offer something to the team, and her early direction, that helped me stay on track.

In latter days, it has been Ben Care who has had a major hand in the formation of all that is here. He has been an excellent sounding board, an uncomplaining reader of numerous drafts and a constant encourager. All combined with a humility that makes him a joy to work with.

I am indeed blessed.

Neil Hudson
Director, the Imagine Project
The London Institute for Contemporary Christianity

Foreword

I hold a number of strong convictions:

1. There is no way to re-evangelize this nation apart from the impact of the daily lives of ordinary, everyday Christians.
2. The ultimate test of the fruitfulness and authenticity of any church, irrespective of its style or tradition, is the quality of disciples it makes. As this book says, 'Making whole-life missionary disciples is the core vocation of the church.'
3. Today's church in the UK has inherited a disastrous split between evangelism and disciple-making, and often reduces discipleship to a narrowly conceived personal piety.
4. Discipleship cannot be taught from a pulpit or in a classroom alone, but is formed through community, and through godly habits, in the practice of mission and in the context of everyday life.
5. We do not yet fully understand how to form whole-life disciples of Jesus in our seductive consumer and celebrity culture.

6. Many of the important things we do understand have been learned through LICC's Imagine Project. Participating in it is a vital way to increase our understanding.

It is thus with both conviction and enthusiasm that I commend Neil Hudson's book. It is rooted in the most foundational of all theological statements: 'Jesus is Lord.' It has been developed from actual practice in partnership with pilot project churches. It recognizes the critical role of the local church, yet it is not about the church for the church's sake, but a church for the sake of the kingdom.

My commendation has to be qualified with a health warning! If you are looking for some quick fixes to make your church better, you won't find them here. (They don't exist.) The purpose of this book is to turn your church inside out.

Graham Cray
Archbishops' Missioner, Leader of the Fresh Expressions team

Beginnings and the bigger picture

This book is about how an ordinary church, your church perhaps, can become a community of people who help one another live out their whole life – at home, at work, in church, in the neighbourhood – as followers of Jesus, engaged in his mission to the world.

'What other kind of church would you really want to be involved in creating?' you might well ask.

Still, whole-life disciple-making churches are in fact rather rare.

You can search out fine preaching churches, and fine churches involved in social action, and churches that really know how to pray, and churches where the worship in music and song is sublime, but it is rare, very rare, to find a church where the main thing is exactly what Jesus identified as the main thing. 'Go and make disciples,' was Jesus' final instruction to the disciples he had made.

He did not say, 'Go and make converts.' He did not say, 'Go and make people who know quite a lot.' He said, 'Therefore go and make disciples of all nations, baptising them in the name of the Father and of the Son and of the Holy Spirit, and teaching them to obey everything I have commanded you' (Matthew 28:19–20). And Jesus had taught his disciples quite a lot about pretty much every area of life. He'd taught them that their mission was everywhere – not just in synagogues and in the temple courts – but everywhere.

A new mission strategy

But that's not the mission strategy we have in the UK church or indeed in the global church. As Mark Greene pointed out at the Third Lausanne Congress for World Evangelisation, on the whole the overall mission strategy of the church worldwide is:

> To recruit the people of God to use some of their leisure-time to join the mission initiatives of church-paid workers.[1]

Of course, this approach to mission has borne fruit in wonder ful ways for all kinds of people: mums and toddlers, teens, the elderly, drug addicts, the homeless, and indeed the people down our street. Praise God for it all. And praise God for the leaders who have envisioned and mobilized their communities to such good effect. But it is still merely a leisure-time approach that only engages the vast majority of Christians in mission in a proportion of their leisure time, and that is in fact a small proportion of their overall time.

What might happen if all of God's people recognized that the whole of their lives mattered to God, not just because he *cares* for them (though, of course, he does) but because these ordinary lives can be directly *involved* in God's mission? What would happen if they realized that their lives are of real significance specifically because of God's desire for the whole world to be reconciled to himself? What would happen if the 98% of Christians who are not in church-paid work were engaged in mission not for three to ten hours a week, maybe 5% of their waking time, but for 100% of their waking time? At the very least, it would change their early morning prayer, wouldn't it?

This book, then, is not just about a minor change of perspective; it's a call to the church to take seriously Christ's call to nurture disciples who are learning to live out the profound implications of following him in every area of their life.

Who do we think you are?

This has been written to encourage church leaders to be courageous in concentrating on the main reasons they are in ministry – to make whole-life disciples. And it's written by a church leader who is still plugging away at this after twenty-five years. So I know that this is not always easy. There are multiple demands on our time, exciting distractions on offer, days of disheartening disappointments that get in the way. But if as leaders we don't embrace this call to whole-life disciple-making, we will turn our backs on the central aspect of our vocation.

But although this is a book for leaders, please don't think it's only for 'full-time' leaders. Leadership has nothing to do with whether you are paid or not. You might be one of the many heroes in local churches who feel an overwhelming loyalty to your congregation and a responsibility for its ongoing spiritual health. You may never have been paid for what you do, and you might be glad that you don't do this 'full-time', but everyone knows your determination. Whatever your situation, the task we are engaged in is to embrace Mark Greene's conclusion in his inspirational essay, *Imagine: How We Can Reach the UK*, and turn it into a reality:

The UK will never be reached until we create open, authentic, learning and praying communities that are focused on making whole-life disciples who live and share the Gospel wherever they relate to people in their daily lives.

This book, then, is not just about helping local churches make whole-life disciples; this book is about reaching the 56 million people in the UK who don't know Jesus.

Turning vision into reality

Still, it is one thing to diagnose a problem, but another thing to present an alternative vision. At LICC we wanted to go further. We wanted to work out how to turn vision into reality – how we could contribute to creating churches full of people who see their whole lives as being able to be used for God's mission and purpose.

So it was that, after extensive research among leaders and congregations, and after many seminars around the country with church leaders of a variety of denominations, we concluded that we needed to work with local churches who wanted to discover how to make whole-life disciples. Over three years we worked with sixteen churches of different sizes from different streams and in different parts of the country. We called it the Imagine Pilot Project.

And as we worked alongside ordinary churches and as we found others who were travelling a similar path, we discovered that it is possible to go from being a good church doing good things to become a church that is focused and fruitful as it pursues its growth as a whole-life disciple-making community. It is possible to become a church that helps others live and share the gospel in all of life.

What it takes to change

It's possible. But it takes persistence and patience. It wasn't a matter of identifying 'five easy steps to missional transformation', or developing a range of foolproof, ready-to-use, 'off the peg' resources that will transform your church by Tuesday fortnight – though we have developed quite a few resources. Rather, we have discovered an organic, catalytic process that could be used by any church, regardless of their denominational stream, their numerical strength, their age profile or their geographical location.

Of course, exactly what any individual church might end up doing will be different. And certainly different churches did things in a different order. Each church is unique. It's not just that they are in particular locations with particular challenges; they also have their own history, and their own diverse mix of people with their specific gifts, talents, life experiences and idiosyncrasies, and they do things in their own particular and sometimes peculiar ways – they speak their very own dialect. Still, the encouraging reality is that God understands their local dialect and he has a way of dealing with every church according to his plans and purposes.

Nevertheless, there are dynamics that we know are effective at enabling a church to create a disciple-making environment, a culture that releases people to live and grow as disciples in the whole of life.

Essentially this change begins to take place when the *whole* church takes seriously the call to live distinctively for Christ wherever they spend time and to recognize that these places will be where they can be shaped by the Spirit, where they can learn to incarnate, to live out and share the truths and wisdom of Scripture.

For this to happen, at least four things need to be achieved. We'll explore them all in more detail but, in summary, there needs to be:

1. a renewed vision of the extent of the Lordship of Jesus and the scope of the mission that he calls us to be involved in;
2. clarity in understanding the relationship between the church in its gathered form (things we do together in a place) and the church in its scattered form (things we do when we are apart from one another);
3. change in the *culture* of the church, otherwise change will not be permanent but just an interesting interlude; and
4. a series of small changes which carry the whole-life DNA and cumulatively have the potential to help sustain a disciple-making emphasis.

We have seen that when this process is followed, people become liberated to recognize that their whole lives matter to God. And when this happens to sufficient numbers of people in a congregation, their life together inevitably begins to feel very different – even if many of the things they do together might look exactly the same.

However, we also had to face the reality that some churches we worked with were not able to change their direction of travel. Similarly, not all the churches saw the outcomes they, or we, had hoped for.

In some cases, they were waylaid by events within their congregations. In other cases, the level of financial and emotional investment in the church building meant they were unwilling to emphasize the missionary life of people away from it. Some of the churches saw the beginnings of the fruit of the process, but then the growth was stunted and failed to flourish fully. Sometimes this was because they were distracted by issues thought to be more urgent. For some there were disruptions in leadership that meant that the central calling of the church received less attention than the activity of ensuring that the community could function together. Such is church life.

But these were valuable lessons in themselves. They provided a dose of reality in the midst of much hope: it is not easy for any community to make the kind of changes that enable people to have a different perspective on their own lives and live them differently. However, if the process is introduced with care and with determination, the results are significant for individuals and church communities and, vitally, for the people they connect to day by day on their frontlines.

This is not the whole story

The remainder of this book is not the whole story of the last few years. It has three aims:

1. to clarify the principles on which the growth of a whole-life disciple-making community must be based;
2. to outline a process that appears to bear fruit for churches who embrace the challenge of enlarging their capacity for mission and discipleship; and
3. to illustrate some of the marks of fruitfulness that a church could expect to see in the early stages if they were to embark on a similar process.

This book, then, is about how to create an environment where disciple-making is central and natural. So it is not about the particular challenges of equipping disciples for their specific mission contexts, nor does it offer an outline of the biblical truths, spiritual disciplines and practical skills that are vital for fruitful living in contemporary society. Those are vital issues, but addressing those without first ensuring that a local church community has created a culture that is committed to whole-life disciple-making is like trying to plant oak trees in sand. You might get one oak, but you certainly won't get a forest.

Along the way we will use two phrases a lot. One of them is 'whole-life discipleship'. In a sense it's a shame that we have felt the need to qualify what we mean by discipleship. But we have used the phrase because we want to make absolutely clear that anything that is in danger of sliding into a sacred–secular divided life (where some things *really* matter to God, and then there's the rest of life) needs to be avoided. As will become clear, Christians use the word 'discipleship' in all sorts of specialized ways: from superior Bible awareness, to specific Christian practices (fasting, Bible reading and so on), to knowing how to behave in Christian contexts such as church. Whole-life discipleship intends to mean what it says: there is no area of a Christian's life that Jesus does not have ownership of, and there is no part of their life that he does not want to use for his glory.

The other recurrent phrase we will use relates to 'mission' or, on occasions, 'missional living'. Most Christians know that mission matters, but many think that it has nothing to do with their ordinary lives. It's easy to think that mission is what happens in 'church time' or is the province of the professionals, those who have it in their job descriptions. Our aim is that everyone, at whatever stage of life they may be, should know that they can be used as part of God's mission, in the places they spend most of their time with non-Christians, and that this mission begins in the everyday life.

Finally, it is important to be clear that this book is not offered as the final answer to all the questions, but rather as a summary of what we and our partners have learned so far. We continue to work with churches, clusters of churches and denominations around the country, and we continue to learn. Our hope is that this publication will be catalytic, that it will generate further experimentation and wisdom within the body of Christ, and that others will share their wisdom with us and the wider body so that together we might help one another keep Jesus' main thing the main thing: to make whole-life missionary disciple-making central and fruitful in the life of the church, for the sake of the nation, for the sake of the world.

*Christianity without discipleship
is always Christianity without Christ.*

Dietrich Bonhoeffer

1

God's people out there:
in place – ready to go?

Then . . .

It was a Wednesday morning around 10.30 am in 2004. I was
a paid leader of a local church and I was sitting in a packed
room full of paid church leaders, listening to Mark Greene
calling for the end to the sacred–secular divide, the belief that
some things, but not all things, really matter to God, a belief
that has plagued the mission fruitfulness of the church. I was
hearing the challenge to get engaged in whole-life disciple-
making and I was imagining what could happen if all the
people in my church could grasp the simple idea that where
they were, at that exact time – around 10.33 by now – could
be the place that God wanted to use them for his kingdom
purposes.

I was hearing all this and I was becoming indignant.

I wanted to defend my past sixteen years in church leadership; I had been trying to do this all along. Internal voices told
me that we were doing all right as we were: growing in

numbers, reaching out to our local community, beginning to see a youth work develop. And yet other voices inside me cheered the message on. I had heard this before, but somehow had never been able to move past good intentions. Could things be different if I were able to gain a new perspective?

I had a prayer meeting planned for the following week, and that was on my mind. Mark asked what we usually prayed for in our church prayer gatherings. Did we only concentrate on the corporate activities of the church: youth work, the children's work, our outreach programmes and the like? Or did we also pray for people where they were: home, work, wherever? The question led to an idea.

Ten days later the prayer meeting took place. I asked three people to talk about their work situations: one was out of work, one loved his job and one person was in a new job. After I'd interviewed them and asked them what they were learning about God and themselves in these situations, we prayed for them. Then we all split up into different areas of the church according to the signs that were displayed around the room: 'I love my job', 'I'd like a new job', 'I wish I still worked' and 'I need to know what to do next'. People talked together, listened to the issues each was facing and prayed for one another.

It was the first church prayer meeting that I had ever led where the agenda had been shaped solely by the everyday experiences of the church members out in their everyday world, rather than simply praying for the activities of the gathered church. Why had it taken so long?

That evening began a process. That simple shift in our prayer meeting demonstrated that we could challenge the old sacred–secular divide, that there was a way forward. I suspect the meeting addressed a suppressed yearning among the church community, a yearning that when we gathered together our activities would be more directly linked to our everyday lives. And it also triggered something in me. I realized that the desire I'd long had that people would be shaped and commissioned to make a difference wherever they found themselves could come true. And that made me realize how strong that desire was in me. It connected to the heart of why I came into the pastoral ministry in the first place.

And now . . .

Shuttle forward five years or so, and I'm sitting in a minister's front room listening to a group of people from one of the churches engaged in LICC's Imagine Pilot Project. I was asking people where they spent most of their time, and what they did with that time.

> In the group was a lady called Isabelle. She was a quiet lady and hadn't contributed much to the conversation thus far. Turning to her, I asked her what she did with her time. She looked very thoughtful. 'I don't know; I've been wondering that while you've been talking. I just clean the house, go to the shops and look after the grandchildren from time to time.' I asked her to tell us more about the grandchildren. She told us that she picked some of them up from school and she told us that her oldest granddaughter came to Sunday dinner most weeks. Often she would ask Isabelle about church and what had been happening. So Isabelle would tell her about the service and the sermon. I asked her what age this grandchild was, expecting her to tell us that she was about ten years old. It turned out she was twenty-two.
>
> The conversation that followed was really interesting. Up until then, the minister had assumed he'd been preaching to a largely elderly congregation, hoping somehow to reach a

younger generation. Suddenly he found out that at least one of his listeners was passing on his sermon to a young twenty-something woman. He began to think about what he might say at 11.30 to Isabelle that would be most relevant to her granddaughter a couple of hours later.

The others in the group had been friends with Isabelle for years. But they had never heard her talk this way about her grandchildren, didn't know their names, and had no idea of the challenges that they might have been facing. So no-one could have prayed for them, nor for the ministry that this grandmother already had in the family.

We stopped, prayed and recommissioned Isabelle back to her family.

A few months later, at the next meeting, I asked her about her grandchildren. 'Well, I don't know what's happening, but my daughter's asking questions about faith and church now. I'm on a bit of a roll.'

And then she added, brilliantly, 'I know what I'm supposed to be doing now.'

This story is important for all sorts of reasons:

- It's significant that Isabelle had been engaged in a meaningful ministry for years, though neither she nor her church realized it.
- She was taken aback by the initial question because no-one had asked it before. And her nonplussed response may well be common. Most people do not think of their everyday lives as being the arena where God will work. Many feel that it might even be big-headed to think that God could use them there.
- It's significant that after we listened to Isabelle's experiences and prayed for her, she had a renewed

confidence in what she was already doing. Most people don't need to be encouraged to do *more*; they just need to see what they do in a different light.

This is a story that has released many other people's imaginations. This unassuming grandmother had thought she had no significance in God's plans or any real missional influence. By 'unearthing' what was already happening, she was able to see that she did have a real area of influence and began to believe that God could use her. Nobody had ever prayed for her about the role she played in her family because no-one knew about it.

How many Isabelles are there in our churches? How many people would find a new energy and confidence if they were able to hear that what they were involved in was significant mission work? Could it be that it is these people who are a key part of the answer to the central mission question that we all face together: 'How will we reach the UK'?

Good news for individuals and churches

My story as a church leader and Isabelle's story share one thing in common: *both* of us had been encouraged to see our lives differently. Change becomes a real possibility when we gain a new perspective on our lives: our lives together as church gathered together, and our lives when we are apart from one another.

We are convinced that God wants to liberate people like Isabelle to embrace their everyday lives for the sake of his mission. This happens on our 'frontlines': the places we are in, with people who do not know Christ and where we accept the responsibility to live as mission agents of the kingdom of God.

However, we know that many simply do not think of their everyday lives through these lenses. Still, to be fruitful out on the frontline over the long haul, people not only need a new set of lenses to see their situations differently; they also need a church community behind them that is committed to helping them be God's people in all of life.

And for that to happen, what is needed is more than some new programme; it's a much more fundamental shift of perspective. It will involve everyone connected to the local church – the church leaders, those responsible for the different departments of the church, the worshipping members of the church. It may begin with a small group of people committed to the cause, but if the change is successful, it will affect everyone's experience of being part of the local church.

This is because what is being proposed is a change of church culture. We need a new culture that changes the way we relate to one another; a culture where our activities help us see the potential for everyday mission; a culture that enables us all to become mature, whole-life followers of Jesus.

Perhaps the easiest way to give an insight into what might be possible for many ordinary churches is to allow people who have been through this process of change to tell their story.

When a church changes

There's a church in Dewsbury who invited LICC to work with them on the Imagine Project. They were a successful church in their town, not a particularly large church, but a strong church aware of the challenge of witnessing to the Christian faith in a place where Islam has a very visible and, at times, aggressive presence.

Their story is one of equipping people to live confidently for Christ when they were not within the perceived safety of their gathered church, when they were scattered across the town Monday to Saturday.

After two years of intentionally concentrating on becoming a whole-life disciple-making community, the pastor was asked to reflect on the culture shift that had happened in the church:

> 'What's changed?' he says. 'Everything has changed, and the biggest change has been in me. I've had to change the most.
>
> 'For many years we have been an "attractional" church. The central focus was on getting people into the church building. And over the years we'd done this well, filling the church building and putting on great services. But gradually we began to realize there was a disconnect between what was happening in the building on a Sunday and what was happening in people's lives during the week. It was as though once we left the building, the really important business was over. I needed to be reminded that for the church members, it was just beginning.'

The fruit of this change of perspective was heard in the conversations that people began to have in the church:

> 'People used to say to me that they loved church, but hated what they do "out there",' he continues, 'but now that has changed. People are saying, "This job is exactly where I'm meant to be. I may not like the job right now, but I'm exactly where God wants me to be and I want to be the best I can be in this place." That is simply because we have heightened the importance of where they are and commissioned them to do it.' This is a vision that runs right through the church, from the very youngest. People are being equipped to go to the places where they already are, whether playgrounds or old people's homes, as missionaries.

Essentially, people in the church began to reclaim their everyday lives as their frontline, the place they could be used by God:

> Peter works for an engineering company. He said, 'You know what a factory is like; the place is filled with lads. I'll go in on a Monday morning and they'll say, "Have you prayed for me this week?", making a joke of it. But now I can say in all seriousness, "Yes, I have."' He goes on, 'I struggle with my boss and sometimes I feel like throwing the towel in or not giving 100% as a Christian. But since this teaching, it's made me realize I've got to do my bit and I just think, "You might not appreciate me, and I sometimes don't like you, but I'm going to give it my 100% anyway because this is where God has called me to be."'

What gave Peter this confidence and such a renewed focus?

One of the significant realities in this church is that everyone was challenged to change – leaders and people. The leaders needed to think about what their fundamental task was and how their work could most help and support the ongoing life of the church when they were scattered through the week. Church members had to think about their motivation for coming to church and building relationships with one another in the light of their responsibilities to the wider world. The results were that people began to see their everyday lives very differently. They began to see that their lives could be used in God's mission.

This was not the end of the journey for that church. It was just the beginning. The challenge for the church was for it to continue to envision people for their ongoing lives – wherever they find themselves. The leaders of the church had to guard against the default setting of the church: to see the 'church sponsored activities' as being of primary importance, rather than the mission potential carried by each individual member.

Two years later, I had the chance to reflect with the church leader on how things had developed further. The past few months had seen a number of mature Christians moving into the area and connecting with the church, including a dietician, a police inspector and a university lecturer. They came with much experience of involvement in church activities and were keen to offer this experience to their new church family. It was one of the housegroup leaders who articulated the church's response well: 'Yes, that's really going to be helpful to us, but there's time for all that; the bigger question is what's God already doing around you and how can we help?'

The dietician, police inspector and university lecturer and the others paused. They'd been presented with a new question, an unexpected question, but a question that marked the new culture they were involving themselves in.

Building something new

All that follows is about change. It's about working towards a new understanding of the ministry of the church. It's not about adding a new programme into a crowded church schedule, or tweaking existing activities; it is about a much more fundamental change of perspective which will lead to different actions and different outcomes from the ones with which most of us have lived. Put simply, it is a call to see the whole of the people of God live out the whole of their lives under the Lordship of Christ for the sake of the wholeness of God's mission for the whole world.

It involves everyone looking at their lives differently. Church leaders need to be willing to be challenged about their funda-mental role in the church community. This may mean *un*learning some things as well as practising new skills. Church members need to be willing to accept a calling to live as whole-life missionary disciples. For many, this will mean accepting new challenges, finding new confidence and learning to approach life differently. This too will mean they have to undergo a similar process of unlearning old practices and acquiring new skills. This is no small task.

There are five guiding assumptions and two fundamental truths that need to be wrestled with and accepted if this new vision is to become a reality. They have been vital for our work with churches, enabling us and them to stay motivated and hopeful in our work. Let's deal with the assumptions first.

Five important assumptions

1. Churches can change

Introducing change within any organization is hard work, and a church is no different. Sometimes it's tempting to believe that rather than trying to change an existing church culture, it'd be simpler to start again. Start again with a fresh set of people who don't have all the expectations of what church should be about. Start again with younger people, or smarter people, or more spiritually aware people. It might be easier; it might not. The fact is, most of us don't have the luxury of starting from scratch. We are where we are. We are with the people that we are with. The big question is: is God still here? If he is, there is hope. If he isn't, then we need to lock the doors and get on with something else.

We have worked on the basis that God is committed by his Spirit to local congregations, and that therefore there is always hope. Though congregations may fear that they are too weak to see anything significant happen, we believe that the only attitude that kills hope is a dogged resistance to change.

2. *Most churches are tired of being criticized*
Most churches are only too aware of their weaknesses, and often feel guilty about the gap between their best intentions and their actual practices. Therefore, rather than simply outlining the problems, we want to help churches discern creative ways to help nurture, equip and sustain whole-life missionary disciples.

If you're sick and in the doctor's surgery, there is a time for diagnosis of your ills. But if all you go away with is regret and guilt about how you allowed yourself to get into this state, then you're in a worse situation than you were when you went in. Then you were just sick. Now you're sick and full of regret.

So instead of endless diagnosis and criticism of existing practice, we need practical steps to move forward and true stories of hope to encourage us on the journey.

3. *Changing church communities isn't easy*
We are all limited by our situations. There are challenges that may not have any easy solutions, or indeed *any* solutions. Often our desire overreaches our abilities. But this does not daunt us; we simply begin the journey realistically. The last thing the church needs is more unrealistic solutions.

We need to start where we are, not where we would like to be. And we start with the people who want to have an integrated life: one where faith and the rest of life connect. It may be you can only find one other person like this. It doesn't matter: begin the conversation with them.

4. *Churches only have so much energy to address issues*
There is an endless list of possible issues that you may feel you need to be involved in. Therefore, choices have to be made. We suggest that establishing disciples of Jesus who understand the implications of this for their whole lives is the

crucial task at this time. If you are going to be involved in this work, you need to be able to harness the energy of the church towards this end. It has to be the one thing that is seen to be the crucial thing. Other concerns may be addressed once this is in process.

5. Change won't happen if everyone thinks all is well
There needs to be a period of discomfort before the need for change is accepted as vital. Leaders need to be uncomfortable believing that church leadership consists of just keeping the programmes running. People need to be frustrated when church life seems to involve merely turning up to services, small groups or Alpha suppers.

If you believe that 'There must be more than this', then you have already begun the journey to change. If you've listened to too many people feeling that faith does not make sense, then this is the wake-up call you have been entrusted with. If you've wondered what difference all the church activities make in the long run, this is the necessary first provocative step that can lead to a wholescale culture shift.

Two absolutely fundamental truths
The final two assumptions are so fundamental that if they are not in place, everything else will come to a shuddering halt. It's easy to gloss over them, but you must not. They lie behind everything else that is suggested. They are not boxes to be ticked off some imaginary spiritual tick-list; they are the blocks on which everything else is built.

1. Jesus is Lord of all
Here's the problem: 'Jesus is Lord' has become a phrase with which we may have become so familiar that it has lost the radical, comprehensive demand that it implies. It is not just a

ceremonial title we give Jesus when we're in a church context. It's a fundamental truth that has direct consequences for the way we live every aspect of our daily lives (Romans 12:1–3; Philippians 2:1–11; Colossians 3:1 – 4:6; 1 Peter 1:3–25).

If we have bowed our knees to him, then we have been enrolled into his cause. We have not become Christians to escape the complexities of the world, nor has Jesus promised to turbo-boost us through the difficult moments of life (Mark 8:34–36; John 16:33).

We have been included in the kingdom of God as citizens of this new kingdom, so that we can live as ambassadors and agents of this alternative kingdom in the very ordinary offices, classrooms and call centres that we call ordinary life (Ephesians 5:21 – 6:9; Colossians 3:18 – 4:1; 1 Peter 2:13 – 3:7).

At times, it will require uncomfortable obedience: obedience to his agenda (Matthew 16:24).

At times, it will call for renewed imagination as we rethink our approach to common challenges (Matthew 17:24–27).

At other times it will call for faith that holds firm to the fact that situations are not relentlessly spinning out of control (John 14:1–4).

At all times it will need us to be aware of our new identity (Matthew 18:18).

And although no Christian will see this as particularly contentious in theory, it is clear that in our Western, democratic, liberal society we struggle to imagine what this sort of kingdom looks like in practice. So as one Christian remarked, 'All this sounds OK in church, but it doesn't work out there, does it?'

How will we help one another to see that he is the Lord, the one and only omnipotent, omniscient Lord, the Lord with an agenda for his world? A Lord who calls people to live out the implications of this Lordship in the whole of their life. This is the core discipleship task for the church. And unless this core fundamental truth is firmly grasped, unless people really believe that Jesus is Lord of all – of every moment, of every place, of every person, of all of life – then the church community will not have the theological foundation or Spirit-empowered motivation to become a whole-life disciple-making church (Colossians 2:9–15).

2. Making whole-life missionary disciples is the core vocation of the church

Most churches would say that they are already involved in discipleship. And they are. Indeed, discipleship may be one of your key values as a church. And if you have the resources, you may even have someone who has the task of coordinating all things discipleship-related. You may have discipleship groups that some people attend, a discipleship course that is highly recommended for everyone. But simply identifying activities as 'discipleship' does not necessarily mean that people are changing.

The call to discipleship has to be accepted as the norm for every Christian. And that has to begin with the understanding that we need to learn how to follow Jesus – it doesn't happen automatically (Ephesians 4:17 – 5:20). After all, unless we are convinced that discipleship is the core vocation of the church, it will stay as something that the 'keen' ones, the 'committed' ones, get involved in. It'll be seen as A-level Christianity, for the ones who are *really* serious about faith, when most of us feel as though we have settled for the GCSE level.

We have to be absolutely convinced that our life together as a church is key to the way that we will be formed as disciples and that this discipleship will be shaped in the arena of our daily lives. This has always been the task for those whose calling it is to nurture disciples; look at the range of issues Paul deals with in 1 Corinthians 5 – 8. The goal of disciple-making is not to make us more adept in church life, nor even more alert to the theological debates that may be raging in church circles. The goal is to enable us to live our lives in a way that reflects our Master's intentions for the world around us.

If we do not keep disciple-making at the centre of all we do, we will simply be sloganeering, and people will be motivated but not properly equipped or supported as they go out to their frontlines.

This is urgent

What cannot happen is that we just continue as we always have done. To do so will only result in spiritual disaster – for the church, and for the people of the UK who need to hear the good news of Jesus.

All our churches need to become what they were intended to be – communities of disciples who are becoming disciple-makers. This needs a patient urgency; urgency because there are millions of people in the UK who need to hear and see the good news of the gospel of Jesus Christ. But it needs to be *patient* urgency – 'Bear in mind that our Lord's patience means salvation' (2 Peter 3:15). The deep culture of most of our churches has centred on concentrating on gathered church activities, at the expense of the experiences of the church in its scattered form. The changes that need to be introduced have to be embedded well so that a new culture can develop. This will take time. Attempts to rush it will either fail or become bullying and manipulative.

Indeed, although we have learned that there are a number of steps along the road towards becoming a whole-life disciple-making church, this is not a programme but rather an organic process. Churches that have joined the journey have not done all the same things in the same order. Their circumstances were inevitably all different, and people have responded differently to different initiatives that have taken the church on a different route to the same destination. And that destination is not a church that runs more smoothly – though it may well do so – but a community that is enabling its people to be faithful and fruitful out in the great mission field of everyday life.

> This whole-life discipleship stuff is getting under the skin a bit – in our midweek prayer meeting one of our ladies prays for the prosperity of the city, then in the following morning leadership prayer meeting there it is again – we're praying for businesses in Milton Keynes, for our unemployed to not just find jobs but know where they are called to serve God and fulfil that calling in his strength. Deloitte's, Ernst & Young, Homes, Milton Keynes' Job Centre, Santander, Alanod, Accenture, MK hospital, Bradwell School, BT, Keune & Nagel, Stowe School, Invensys plc . . . Lights are on; salt is getting some taste to it!
> Church leader

Pause for thought

1. How would you want to offer help to Isabelle or Peter? What do you imagine would be most helpful to them?
2. What would get in the way of your church embracing the call to become a whole-life disciple-making church?
3. What would need to change? What would this change cost?
4. Where is your primary frontline? What opportunities do you have there to live as a missionary disciple?
5. What would help you live more fruitfully?

Further reading

Chester, Tim and Timms, Steve, *Everyday Church* (Inter-Varsity Press, 2011).

Cray, Graham, *Disciples and Citizens* (Inter-Varsity Press, 2007).

Greene, Mark, *Imagine: How We Can Reach the UK* (LICC, 2003).

Ogden, Greg, *Transforming Discipleship* (Inter-Varsity Press, 2003).

Peterson, Eugene, *Christ Plays in Ten Thousand Places* (Eerdmans, 2005).

Willard, Dallas, *The Divine Conspiracy* (Fount, 1998).

Willard, Dallas, *The Great Omission* (HarperCollins, 2006).

While we are concerned that people come to the church,
we have not thought deeply enough about what they will become
in time within the church . . . our commission is to disciple
nations, not merely to draw large crowds to ourselves.

J. I. Packer and G. Parrett,
Grounded in the Gospel

2

The whole-life church:
a renewed vision

I spend a lot of my time talking to church leaders and I've grown used to receiving a certain look. It happens in the following conversation. I begin talking about the need for the people of God to be equipped for mission and to be formed as disciples of Jesus. At this point I'm met with nods of agreement: we share common hopes. However, once I begin to talk about releasing the people of God to engage in mission where *they are already*, rather than just encouraging involvement in the joint mission activities of the church, I'm met with the look.

It's a look of concerned suspicion. The concern is there because leaders are only too aware of the many areas of church life that need involvement. Their fear is that if people are encouraged to take mission seriously in their everyday lives, they'll stop being involved in church activities and it's already hard enough to run all the activities to which they are committed. The suspicion is there because they think I am saying that the local church doesn't matter and that people don't need to be committed to it.

They're right to be aware that a change of perspective is being suggested. They're wrong to think that I'm suggesting that belonging, and contributing, to the life of a local church community is insignificant. It's not.

They're right to think that I am suggesting that the primary mission will be done in the places we spend most of our time. They're wrong to believe that I don't think that mission done as part of teams from the local church is important. It is.

But there has to be more – ministry has to include life together and life when we are apart from one another. And getting the balance between these two aspects of life has been difficult for some leaders to grasp.

The reality is that if you are a church leader, the activities of the gathered church take up most of your time, emotions and energy. And it's easy to imagine that everyone else feels the same. It's always disappointing when you realize they don't. While people may feel a real sense of commitment and belonging to the church community, this is not where most of them spend most of their time. Most of the time they are separated from one another: they are the scattered church. And it's family, work, neighbours, finances or the future that takes their time and energy.

Nevertheless, when they are scattered, they are still the church; they are still members of the body of Christ – even if they are alone; they are still called to be the individual representatives of his body, wherever they are.

Church is not something we do; it's who we are.

The problem has been our understanding of the relation-ship between our times as church together and our times as church apart. Traditionally when we have been together, we have spent most of our time encouraging one another to con-centrate on the gathered activities of church life. This is obviously significant, but has meant that we have limited our understanding of church to a particular place, time and set of activities.

This creates the impression that the most likely way that we will serve God, or make a difference in the world, will be primarily through the activities of the 'official church pro gramme'. What we do at work, with friends, in clubs, activities and other communities can easily be ignored.

What you might be missing

If we only concentrate on our activities together, we might be missing the significant mission that is already happening. Because we focus on hearing about the plans and fruitfulness of our gathered church mission, we might miss the chance to celebrate far more often. We saw this clearly in one of the churches we worked with.

> They are an average size church with a consistent, generous, active and fruitful ministry working among the poorest people in Manchester. They give away tens of thousands of pounds each year to agencies working with the poor, and many of their own ministries concentrate directly on ministering to the poor.
>
> At one gathering of leaders, I was asking about the heroes of the church and who were most likely to be invited to share their stories of what God was doing. It's not surprising that for them it was those who were working with the poor.
>
> What was interesting was the remark made by one of the leaders' wives who was at the meeting. She was a doctor, working in one of the poorest wards in the city, dealing in a professional capacity with some of the very same people to whom members of the church were ministering directly in their spare time.

It had just dawned on her that she'd never been invited to speak about her work. It hadn't been seen as the church at work – even though she in fact probably spent more time with the poor than anyone else in the congregation. It was just her job.

This church had a tradition of encouraging people to tell their stories in small groups, and people being able to ask the leaders for permission to share their experiences in the Sunday worship gathering. However, there is a marked difference when someone is invited to speak. An invitation from the leaders gives the speaker explicit validation. If the only invited stories are the stories of the church ministry teams, people can quickly draw conclusions as to the roles that are most valued.

The leaders of the church took the challenge offered to them and began to ask a wider range of people to share their stories with the congregation in an attempt to explicitly change their culture's heroes.

Let me emphasize what was happening here:

- The church was doing a great work with the poor.
- The church had a wider vision than its own comfort.
- The church was willing to put its money where its compassion was.
- The church welcomed stories from those working in church-sponsored activities.

But:

- The church already had access to people in difficult life-situations through the jobs of some of their people.
- These people were living out the life of the kingdom.
- The practices of the church didn't help either those involved or the wider church see this reality.

The important point we want to make here is not that some things shouldn't be done by the gathered church, or in its name. They simply need to take their place alongside the activities that all the church members are involved with throughout the week. The result is not that mission activity will be diminished; on the contrary, it will be seen to be so much more diverse, effective and frequent than we might have imagined.

If the question 'How will the UK be reached?' is going to be addressed successfully, then we have to recognize that the most realistic way that this will happen is by re-envisioning God's people to live authentic Christian lives in the places where they already find themselves, wherever these may be. They are the places where a different way of living can be demonstrated, a different way of dealing with the past, a different way of accepting the uncertainties of the future.

The challenge for us all

There has been a range of innovative approaches to church over the past decade or so. Many people have set out to rethink what we mean by church. They have experimented with new forms of existing church, new forms of church planting and new forms of church for the de-churched, the un-churched, the never-thought-about-it-churched.

However, whatever form the church takes, in whatever ways different people come to belong to the community, they will all face the same central issue: how do we ensure that our life together equips us for our life when we are separated from one another? How do we make whole-life disciples?

So it doesn't matter if you are:

- a traditional church, a middle-of-the-road church or a new church;

- a fresh expression, a mission-shaped community or a new monastic;
- a cathedral, a community or a chapel;
- a preaching centre, a worship centre or a prayer centre;
- Soul Survivor, Keswick or Walsingham;
- post-evangelical, post-charismatic or neo-reformed;
- urban, suburban or rural.

Wherever you fit in the spectrum, the challenge remains: how does what we do 'in here' enable people to live for Christ 'out there'?

The challenge of the biblical big story

The Bible gives us a revelation of a God who is not only the Creator of all things and the Redeemer of all things, but a God interested in every aspect of life. Yet often our preaching and teaching in church has come to suggest that the primary place God acts in power is in the gathered church or in the activities of the gathered church's ministries in the neighbour-hood or local community. However, even a cursory glance at Scripture suggests a different story. It is a story of God's intention to dwell with humanity. The story begins with God talking with humans in a garden (Genesis 3:8), finds its climax in a city in which God dwells among redeemed humanity (Revelation 21:3–4) and has as its central crux, in every sense of that word, the incarnation of the one known as 'Immanuel' – God with us (Matthew 1:23).

God with his people. But where? Yes, God is with his people in gathered worship. It is important – a large part of the book of Exodus is taken up with the plans for the tabernacle, the portable meeting place with God, and then the actual building of the structure. But God is clearly also at work away from this site. He is the God who miraculously provides food and water in inhospitable deserts, defeats enemies and provides laws that will create a nation. All the way through Scripture we see God at work more often away from the sites of worship, whether they be tabernacles, temples, synagogues or churches, than inside them. This people is given a land to live in, laws by which to live, rulers to lead them, worship spaces to focus on and a destiny to fulfil. It is noticeable that this encompasses all their lives – not just the 'gathered worship' part. However, the mission of the gathered people of God is important. God is concerned that a people should be formed who will be the means of blessing to the whole world (Genesis 12:2–3).

Indeed, the biblical story is not about God's concerns solely for a proportion of humanity that will come together to worship him; his concern is that these people will carry his cause into the whole world. And when the people of God concentrate solely on themselves, they run the risk of his judgment. As Christians, we are called into a community of fellow believers so that together we might display the realities of the kingdom of God in and to the world.

However, not all mission is corporate mission. The New Testament portrays the followers of Jesus as either itinerant missionaries pressing on to the next town or city, or people in those cities figuring out how to work (Colossians 3:22–25), what to do in marriages (1 Corinthians 7), what to eat (Romans 14) and how to live as public citizens (1 Peter 2) now that they had a new identity in Christ. Most of the concerns of the epistles reflect this call to be discipled in order that the public life of Christians would be marked by a sense of the purpose of God for his whole world.

So why do we read Scripture through a lens that assumes that gathered church is the most significant location for God to work in and through people? I want to suggest that we have not taken sufficient account of the radical differences between a local church today and a local church in the first century. These differences are not necessarily good or bad but they do highlight some of the dynamics that may have led to our contemporary emphasis on the gathered church. I've highlighted in the following table the implications of four situations that we have generally taken for granted in our life together in our churches.

The situation in the early church	Our situation	Our possibilities	Potential positive effects	Potential negative effects
They used private homes (Acts 18:7; Romans 16:5, 23; 1 Corinthians 16:19; Colossians 4:15; Philemon 2).	We use public buildings.	Mission activities can be offered from the building; large numbers of people can be catered for.	It can become a hub for a local community. It is a clear reference point for the community. A range of activities can be offered.	Buildings take up a lot of financial resources. Activities need a constant flow of volunteers. The more successful an activity is, the greater the call for paid employees to run it.

So when we read about the church being involved in mission, and encourage one another to get involved and pray that we might be effective, our first reaction is to think about how we can do this from our facilities. This inevitably means that we can think of mission as being primarily 'gathered-church', church-sponsored mission.

The practice of the early church	Our situation	Our possibilities	Potential positive effects	Potential negative effects
It was not automatically assumed that church leaders would be paid (Acts 18:1–4; Philippians 4:10–13; 2 Thessalonians 3:6–10).	Generally, we assume that for a church to thrive we need (a) paid leader(s).	We have people who are free to concentrate on church affairs and can represent the church to the local community.	They can open up mission opportunities in the local neighbourhood. They can identify the resources within the church community.	It can be seen as 'their job' to do the work of mission in the church's name, so no-one feels the need to be involved. Or they can innovate so many mission possibilities that these become an unrealistic drain on people's leisure-time availability.

So as leaders become known in the area as people who care for the neighbourhood and have time to be involved in activities, they can spot the opportunities that are available to 'make a difference'. Because these may be neighbourhood based and need people to be available, the minister then has to recruit for the activities, or get involved himself because there is no-one else available. Some people will think this is a good use of the leader's time; others will want to support him or her, but will need to use their leisure time to do so since this is away from their ordinary 'everyday' lives.

The experience of the early church	Our experience	Our possibilities	Potential positive effects	Potential negative effects
Unless they were rich, people did not have 'time off' in the same way as we understand it in the West.	We have a lot of leisure time.	People can get involved in activities outside their employment situations, and indeed often want to.	The church has a rich resource of local volunteers.	We can give the impression that this time is the most significant missional time for people.

So because people do have leisure time, and because some people find their everyday frontlines tedious or difficult, they can prefer to engage in mission in these leisure times. This can mean that they see their everyday locations as secondary places of mission, or worse, distractions from the work that they would really like to be involved with.

The context for the early church	Our situation	Our possibilities	Potential positive effects	Potential negative effects
They were viewed with suspicion at best, persecuted at worst (1 Peter 2:13–25; 3:8 – 4:19).	We live in a largely benign society.	We can offer services to the community around us and people will use them.	We can serve the vulnerable and demonstrate the reality of the gospel.	We can underestimate the cost involved in living as whole-life disciplemakers.

So it is easy to come to believe that the cost of our discipleship relates to the demands on our time and money – our involvement rather than the more radical cost of recognizing that living as disciples of Christ will call for different approaches to the whole of life. So we can ignore the implications of the Lordship of Christ on our work or on our social aspirations, for example.

Why a new perspective matters

It can be tempting for some to recognize the problem of the traditional emphasis on gathered church activities and swing the pendulum to the opposite spectrum where there would be no significance in gathering together. This would be a fundamental error. The truth is that we need to have a clear idea of why we are part of gathered church and a clear sense of our life in the scattered mode of church and a clear understanding of how they connect with each other. They both matter.

1. A new perspective reminds us why the gathered church is so important

The community of the church is one of the primary contexts in which God's people learn a new framework for life. Salvation, our surrender to the Lordship of Christ, involves change. Some of this happens supernaturally through the work of the Spirit, but some change can only happen in the context of relationships with others. Our life as church together should be one of the primary arenas whereby we are shaped into our new life as disciples of Jesus.

This seems to have been the primary task of the apostle Paul as he discipled the early Christians. Of all the churches that Paul had to deal with, nowhere was more problematic than the church community in Corinth. Having been thoroughly shaped by their culture, the Corinthians appeared to struggle to know how to live as people who were being shaped by Christ. They were fractious, obsessed with celebrity, fearful of losing face, and selfish worshippers. Essentially they were no different from their pagan neighbours. Other than that, they were a great church.

Paul's task was to help them recognize what life should

be like as people following Jesus. In the midst of all the various problems that he has to untangle, he needs to ensure that they understand their fundamental identity in Christ, and know how that will shape their actions in their real world.

1. He urges them to recognize that they are the **recipients of grace** (1 Corinthians 1:2–9, 26–31).
2. He centres their life together as believers by **remembering the gospel story** (1 Corinthians 1:18 – 2:4; 15).
3. He encourages them to **relate to one another** as members of God's new family (1 Corinthians 3; 4; 12 – 14).
4. He calls them to **respond to the gospel in love and service** (1 Corinthians 16).

Paul's concern is that the Corinthians' security of knowing who they were in Christ, their fundamental identity, would be lived out in the midst of a cosmopolitan city that largely saw the message of Christianity as irrelevant.

Our task is exactly the same. It is in our gatherings with fellow believers that we understand who we are, how we are to act and the story that we live in. The surrounding culture will always pull us in different directions. We need our life together to remind us of who we are in Christ.

2. A new perspective reminds us why the scattered church is important

For too long we have emphasized a false picture of the church's current and potential missionary activity. For example, many people see the church represented by the black dots in the diagram below.

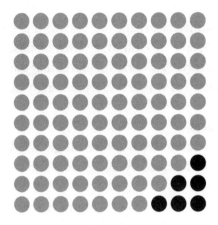

They think of the church as in the corner, in the ghetto, irrelevant, under siege, struggling to make connections with wider society, working hard to reach people, investing much time, effort and resources in mission work, but often failing to make any real impact.

But most of the people of God, most of the time, are not in the corner or in the ghetto. Most of the time the people of God are scattered out in the world, connecting to scores of people in an average week – connecting with work colleagues, family members, neighbours and friends. The reality is more like this:

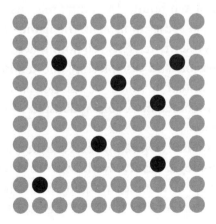

If we let this simple fact shape our disciple-making, this would result in the people of God living lives of mission, commissioned into all sorts of wonderful places that the 'ministers' of the gathered church would find frustratingly inaccessible.

Times and places

However, the relationship between the gathered and scattered church is not just shaped by 'place'; it is also shaped by time.

There are	168	hours in a week.
Let's assume	48	hours are spent sleeping.
That leaves	120	hours.
Most people can give	10	hours per week, maximum, to church activities (unless they are employed by a church or have a lot of voluntary time).
That leaves	**110**	**hours per week for work, family and leisure.**

A maximum of ten hours. Ten hours that may be worship, small group and some ministry in the name of the church. But 110 hours elsewhere. This 110-hour space is our primary arena for mission and discipleship; the ten-hour space is the primary context in which we can not only worship and pray to God together, but equip and inspire one another for ongoing mission.

So the question is: how can we best use the ten hours (fewer for many people, in reality maybe two to three hours per week) that we spend together to equip one another to live well for Christ in the other 110? If we really grasped that we have a limited amount of time together, but that this time really mattered, that this time was going to be a crucial part of the equipping of the people of God, what would change?

- What would we pray for when we were together?
- How could preaching really help us live well for Christ, wherever we were?
- What issues would be given most time in leadership meetings?
- What songs would worship leaders choose?
- What would we talk about in small groups?
- What stories would we expect to hear when we came together?

We would use our time with a different intent. We would have different conversations. We would have different criteria for deciding if we had had a good time together. And it would change because we had developed a fresh vision of our calling to mission in the 110.

Whole-life calling and frontline mission

Many of the stories in this book so far are actually about people discovering that they had a context for mission, a frontline, where they already spent time – a grandmother, realizing the ministry to her granddaughter; a young factory worker clocking how God could use him in a factory; or a church leader seeing how significant people's workplaces might be.

By the term 'frontline', we mean the place where we realize God's calling to engage with non-Christians in mission. Of course, we are called to be missional in all of life, and called to grow in godliness wherever we are, but usually there's a particular place or group of people that we sense God is guiding us to bless and reach out to. They are often in the place where we spend most of our time – school, work, neighbourhood, a gym, a club. Not always though – one person discovered that her mission field was the local Costcutter supermarket. It was small enough that she could get to know the staff at the tills. It was quiet enough at certain times for her to talk to them. She was a regular enough customer to build relationships there.

Of course, throughout our lives these places will change – school, college, university, work, home, neighbourhood – but regardless of age, marital status, employment status, health and region, we will always have a frontline context where we engage purposefully in mission with those who don't know Jesus.

And it is in these everyday places that the drama of the kingdom of God and the Lordship of Jesus plays out against a prevailing culture that offers disorientated people anaesthetics to stop them thinking about the big issues of life and faith. It's hard to follow the carpenter from Nazareth when your head is full of celebrity shenanigans. But the gospel offers disciples the prospect of God's rule being worked out in the homes, offices, neighbourhoods, towns and cities of everyday lives. These places may or may not be deemed to be significant by the rest of society, but they are to the kingdom of God.

This is the task at hand for all those who are part of the church: to encourage one another not to fall into an easy retreat from the frontlines to the safety of church activities. If we lose the ground here, how will the kingdom of God advance?

The question for every Christian becomes: what does it mean for me to live fruitfully here?

If we take this seriously, then it will affect our prayers, our actions and reactions to events, and our hopes. Christians in days gone by had a way of explaining this sort of life. They encouraged people to believe that they had a vocation, and that they had to embrace it. It's the tragedy of the Christian church that vocation has often been limited to the work of the clergy rather than the calling of everyone.

For some, 'vocation' feels too big a word for what they find themselves doing day by day. Where is the vocation in driving a bus? What is the vocation in being a traffic warden? Where's the honour of a vocation when you serve in a supermarket? What's so special about being a mother or a grandmother that warrants someone to believe it's a vocational task? And what happens when you retire; what does vocational living mean at this stage of life?

The answer to all these questions is found in going back to the meaning of the word itself. Its most basic meaning is the idea of having a call. And linked to that was a sense that you might feel a calling to a certain profession. But what if, for the Christian, the primary vocation, the primary calling, is not in regard to employment but to Christ? Our primary vocation is to be a disciple, an agent of the kingdom.

Isn't it possible that while we might not have chosen to work in a supermarket because it was the most fulfilling job on earth, it has become a vocational space for us who are working for a higher purpose? This is how Paul helped slaves make sense of their situations (Colossians 3:22–25).

In this way of thinking, our situations become a place where we live out the calling that God has for us. We self-consciously find ways of inviting God into those situations. One person doing that was John.

John was working as an assistant in an educational unit that dealt with children with severe behavioural problems. He was a Christian and wanted to live as a whole-life missionary disciple. So he was reliable, honest, trustworthy and hard-working. But these are basic expectations of all the staff; you don't need to be a Christian to live like that. So he faced the question of how he could make a difference where he was, on his frontline.

The problem was that because of the nature of the work, for most of the time he was with just one child. He didn't have much to do with the staff, because it was his job to accompany 'his' child at break-times and lunchtimes. He couldn't talk about his faith at all; that would have been inappropriate. So he did the only thing he could. He prayed for the child throughout the day, every day, for a whole school year. And he believed. He believed that not only would God hear his prayer, but that God would bless the child he was working with.

John did what he could. And what he could do was a lot.

Being discipled in the 110

The 110 is, however, not just the place where we are called to live faithfully and fruitfully. It's also the place that provides an opportunity for us to be shaped. It's the arena for us to be formed as disciples of Jesus.

Family life may not be perfect. Work colleagues may not appreciate our contribution. Friends might let us down from time to time. And any or all of this can have a negative effect on us. The question is, how will we react? Our first reactions may be annoyance, indignation, hurt, resentment. These are not surprising emotions; most people would accept them as natural. But there is a deeper opportunity here: what is Jesus, our discipler, seeking to teach us through it all? How might these situations allow us to be more Christ-shaped, more cross-shaped? Is there not a real possibility that these experiences will encourage us to grow in the fruit of the Spirit, enable us to develop 'unnatural' reactions to the irritations of life, rather than becoming diminished by the challenges?

It is in the midst of these experiences that we will learn what it means to be a follower of Jesus. It is here that we will learn much about the grace of God. It is here that we will experience forgiveness. It is here that we will demonstrate the indwelling stamina that the Spirit offers. We have been called into the kingdom, and are being encouraged and taught to live in a radically different way from the old way of life we were used to. This way of life is not natural. It is the way of Jesus.

We need to learn to practise it. And the role of the gathered church is not only to be a community in which we are envisioned and equipped for the challenges of the 110 and have an opportunity to reflect and pray about them, but also the context where we have the opportunity to learn, practise and develop the skills and attitudes of the maturing disciple that we use in all of life – church and away.

So, for example, where will we learn how to really forgive? New Christians will be introduced to this essential Christian practice in church. They will be reminded of the centrality of forgiveness, and encouraged to receive it from God and extend it to others and they would learn how to do that when, for example, when their relationships in the church are disrupted. In so doing, they will learn a new way of responding, where they might previously have retreated into indignant judgment.

But where will they have the most opportunities to *practise* this new art of forgiveness? Hopefully there will be far more scope for this in the 110 than in the ten. When somebody wrongs them at work, what they need from their fellow Christians is not just prayer and sympathy: they need someone to remind them that this is an opportunity to learn about forgiveness. So their discipling will continue and they will learn the value of the 110 for their growth as Christians. And of course, the other fruits of the Spirit – self-control, patience, kindness and the rest – will develop in the same way.

This has to be real; it's all too easy for this to collapse into pious hopes. It has to be worked out by the father who is struggling to keep his cool with teenagers who are testing the limits of acceptable behaviour, by exhausted young parents struggling to keep working while enduring another night when the children won't sleep, by people hanging on to sanity and self-worth in jobs that threaten to rob them of both, by people frightened by the last medical consultation they've just had. We are all there somewhere – it's just life. But for the Christian, there's more to life than gritting your teeth and bearing it. It's recognizing that the God who is fervently committed to us, and who continues to give himself to us, is able to use these and many other situations to change us to become more than we might have been.

Maybe this is part of what Paul saw when, after outlining the characteristics of the fruit of the Spirit, he encourages those who are 'spiritual' to gently restore someone who is caught in sin (Galatians 6:1). The chapter division doesn't help here; it's easy to think that Paul has moved on to a new topic. The Spirit does bear fruit in our lives, but we need one another to be fruitful. Living by the Spirit and being in mutually accountable relationships may be one and the same thing for those wanting to grow as Jesus-followers.

The '110' is absolutely crucial to our understanding of how God wants to use us, and our awareness of how we can grow as whole-life disciples.

In sum, whole-life discipleship is not only about releasing people for the sake of God's mission, though, of course, it does include this. It is about recognizing that we can be shaped in the whole of life to grow into maturity as the people of God. It should lead to a different perspective on the whole of life.

What's the goal?

The goal of all this is that the community of God's people – in both its gathered and scattered mode – can commit itself to growing as whole-life missionary disciples. This call to be a whole-life disciple is not some elitist form of Christianity. It's just taking seriously the call to follow Jesus in the everyday lives we are already living.

And this life is the ordinary life. By now it should be clear that we are convinced that it is imperative that people are able to own their everyday lives as the arena where God can work in and through them.

This message is hugely liberating for people. In our experience there are many people sitting in churches up and down the country wondering why they are there. They are committed to Christ, and committed to a strong belief in church, but they just wonder why their two worlds seem so disconnected. To begin to reorient their activities so that they can be envisioned to live a full, whole Christian life is what many people have longed for.

It will stop people arriving at retirement full of regret about what they might have missed while they were at work. Hope fully, there will be a generation of people who will know that their work mattered, that in terms of God's work in the world it counted.

Before we begin to suggest the route towards change, there needs to be a moment where the 'pain' of the current situation is able to be identified. This may well be a pain felt by leaders as much as people. Many leaders feel a creeping sense of unreality and long for the same connectedness of whole-life Christianity. New vision needs to be expressed, but also needs to challenge the existing expectations of life and church. The courageous will encourage this to happen, being willing to identify the aspects of the existing culture that are likely to get in the way of lasting change.

But before this begins, there are challenges that can threaten to neutralize any desire to change. I've found that people quickly grasp this need for a broader vision of the Lordship of Christ and the need to have a renewed vision of the relationship between the gathered and scattered church. However, the truth is that in many places the culture of the church is so deeply ingrained in sacred–secular thinking and an over-emphasis on gathered church activities that only a concerted determination to address this culture will result in any lasting change. It's this issue of identifying a church's culture that we will address next.

Our church has changed in a good way. It's more obvious now that it's not just about us, but about everybody else. So people are not coming to church just thinking, 'I need to do this, I need to have this done to me,' but instead come with other people and situations in mind.
Member, Imagine Pilot Church

Since we've concentrated on whole-life issues, the health of the church has become more important than its numerical growth. Numbers were really important to me. How many people turned up told me what I was like and my ability as a pastor. And I can still hear that at the back of my mind. But now I'm more bothered about whether we have done what we can to help people live as fruitful disciples right now.
Leader, Imagine Pilot Church

Pause for thought

1. What difference would it make to your church life if the ten hours of your life together were focused on helping people live as whole-life disciples in the 110?
2. What difference would it make to your church life if the issues faced in the 110 were more evident in the ten hours of gathered church life?
3. What would need to change for this to become a reality?

Further reading

Frazee, Randy, *The Connecting Church* (Zondervan, 2001).
Hauerwas, Stanley and Willimon, William, *Resident Aliens* (Abingdon, 1993).
Hirsch, Alan and Debra, *Untamed: Reactivating a Missional Form of Discipleship* (Baker, 2010).
Stott, John, *The Living Church* (Inter-Varsity Press, 2007).

[The best culture-changers] bear no banners;
they sound no trumpets. Their ends are sweeping,
but their means are mundane. They are firm in their
commitments, yet flexible in the ways they fulfill them.
Their actions may be small but can spread like a virus.
They yearn for rapid change but trust in patience.
They often work individually but pull people together.
Instead of stridently pressing their agenda,
they start conversations.
Rather than battling powerful foes,
they seek powerful friends.
And in the face of setbacks they keep going.

Debra Meyerson,
'Radical Change, the Quiet Way',
Harvard Business Review, 2002

3

Changing from the inside out:
values before actions

It's at this stage that you might expect me to describe the programme of activities that you need to roll out. Indeed, many of us who are activists by nature and pragmatists by persuasion may find ourselves demanding: 'What can we introduce next week (or month, if we are exercising the gift of patience) that will address the problems?' We look for resources, a plan, a programme that can be implemented immediately.

Years ago, church growth was being talked about everywhere. There didn't seem to be a leadership gathering where we weren't motivated, encouraged and challenged to be leaders of growing churches. We were introduced to leaders of churches that had grown from six family members to a crowd of a thousand in less than a year. I guess these leaders were flown in from around the world to encourage us to go and do likewise. Let me assure you, it wasn't encouraging and we didn't do likewise.

One of the countries that received a lot of attention was South Korea. Against a backdrop of struggle, the churches there had seen many come to know Christ. As a minister of a church of around fifty members, afflicted with personal delusions of grandeur and spurred on by inspirational speakers who urged us to 'dream big dreams', I whiled away idle moments imagining what it would be like to lead a church that had as many members as my city had inhabitants.

So when the chance came to go and listen to the minister of the world's largest church, I was keen to find out what would make the difference. And I was more than slightly disappointed to be told that what had happened in their church was that he had built the church around the ministry of women and prayed.

Our church would have fallen apart years ago if the women hadn't been doing all that they were. And we'd tried prayer! Was that all he could offer? Surely there was something else.

I'm wiser now and, along with those who have been involved in the world of pastoral ministry for any time at all, I know there is not a programme out there that will miraculously transform a congregation.

Indeed, as we have worked with different churches, one of the things that they have actually appreciated is that there is no generic programme that all have to follow. But there is a dynamic process. And it is important to see that the two are different. A programme assumes that there is some external resource that, if only we'd accessed it previously, would have prevented our problems. A process looks at the situation as it is, methodically asking questions that open up possibilities unique to our situation.

What is the real issue?

It's crucial that we name the real issues before we attempt to introduce change. We might ask the following questions.

- Have churches been using inadequate resources, and do they just need new, improved discipling programmes?
- Are people uninformed about the missional implications of their faith, and so need more education or motivation?
- Do we need more enlivening worship or more inspiring sermons?

You may have answered some of these questions with a resounding 'Yes'. These may be problems in individual cases, but overall the real issue is that we need a culture change. It's not a lack of knowledge, or inadequate resources, or a lack of inspiration; it's the fact that the deeply in-grained habits and practices of the church have worked against liberating the people of God for whole-life dis-cipleship. Plugging the gap with another programme won't necessarily be effective at changing the culture of the church.

This is why many attempts to change things in church fail. It's not because we lack the resources or the arguments; it's because the 'way we do things round here' has real power.

I'm sure I don't have to defend this diagnosis. But some people in church have an inherent mistrust of anything that sounds like business jargon. They may be wearied by their experiences at work, or just cautious of any approach that might begin to leave God out of the equations. They would be right to be cautious, but wrong to recognize the significance of how church cultures are formed and how they shape our actions and reactions.

Reading between the lines of the letters in the New Testament allows us to see something of the distinctive identity and character of the various churches – their flaws as well as their faithfulness. Among other matters, the New Testament authors tackle this issue of the 'culture' of a church, and are not slow to suggest where it needs changing.

Nowhere is this more evident than in the seven letters to the seven churches in modern-day Turkey in Revelation 2 – 3. When John was looking across the waters from the lonely island of Patmos, he didn't see churches that were doing OK but just needed a bit of polishing to become perfect. He saw churches that had allowed sub-Christian practices to become normal (Revelation 2:14–15, 20–23) and churches with attitudes that meant that the Spirit was not free to use them for the sake of God's purposes (2:4; 3:1–2, 15–17).

Although this had led to different problems in each of the churches, in each case it was breeding a culture that was counter to the gospel. So the remedy had to be decisive. The call to these churches was to wake up (3:2), to repent (2:5, 16, 22), to turn from one way of living and embrace a new way of being the church of Christ in their place. The one who stood at the door wanted to be invited to enter so that his presence might shape their life together – their church 'culture' – in a way that would enable them to bear fruit as his followers.

He still does.

What do we mean by culture?

If you're part of any group, organization or family, you may find that you're the least able to describe accurately your own culture. Culture's like the air we breathe. We take no notice of it most of the time. We've got more important things to do.

But every now and again, you are reminded that things you take for granted are not the same the world over. And you don't have to move far to realize that. Thirty years ago, two hundred miles did it for me: from Halifax, the centre of my universe, to London, a small village in the south. They did lots of things differently there, even mealtimes. I had dinner in the middle of the day. They had it at my teatime. And they didn't seem to think that an invitation for tea involved anything other than a drink. A bitter disappointment to be invited to come for tea and have a cup of tea – that would never have happened in Halifax!

You understand your culture better when you begin to see church through the eyes of visitors. What happens at the church door? When people are arriving, whom do they meet there? What do they receive? What are they asked? Do they know where to go next? What are they given to read? How many people do they get to meet? Do they get a warm welcome and are they then left to sit alone while people prepare for the service? How do they know where to sit?

And does the welcome give an accurate impression of the culture you would want to be true of your church? Or does it depend on who is on the rota?

You get the idea.

So what is culture and how can you discern your own culture? A simplified picture of the views of many writers can be illustrated in the following way.

The Beliefs We Share:
'Everyone knows that'

The Things We Do:
'It's the way we do things around here'

This Is Who
We Are

The Way We
Say Things:
'It's our accent'

The things we do

The expected, and accepted, behaviour of any group becomes less noticeable the longer you have been part of a group. We will all have stories of being caught unawares when someone asks, 'Why do you do that?'

So why do most churches meet together on a Sunday morning around 10.30–11am? Why do they have a collection taken up during the service? Why does communion involve minute pieces of bread/wafer? Why is sixty to ninety minutes seen as the normal length of a service? Why do we sing so much? Why does one person get to speak uninterruptedly for twenty to thirty minutes? Why do we hear so little about everyday life in church? Why do the songs we sing seem so disconnected from our time and place? Why do people who are under stress in their everyday lives feel as though there's nowhere they can talk about it in church circles?

In most cases, there's nothing inherently wrong with these activities. It's just that most of them take place week by week without anyone ever really questioning them, or even wondering why it's 'the way we do things round here'.

Throughout this book there are a number of changes in activities that we have seen have made a difference in the culture of a local church. But let me offer a small change that would signal a major shift in the expectations of people in a local church.

When new people begin attending an average local church, there is a period of settling in, when they decide whether this is going to be the place for them and a time for the church family to get to know them. During this time, there will be a chance for a conversation with them. If they are Christians who have moved from another church, part of that conversation will be about how they might get involved in the life of the church.

Indeed, the conversation may even begin with the words, 'We wondered how we might best use you? Do you work with children, have you an up-to-date CRB, do you play a musical instrument, do you like cleaning church halls, have you always hoped that someone would ask you to wash up after church?' and so on. If they decline all these exciting opportunities, we assure them that they have a nice smile and we recruit them to the welcome team. It's important that they feel that they have something to offer, and we do need help.

But what would a different question reveal about a change in the culture of a church? What would be signalled by the question, 'We were wondering where God is already using you and how we might be of help to you?' Suddenly, even if they don't know how to answer the question, they will know this is a church that has a different view of its ministry.

The way we say things

One of the joys of living on a small island like Britain is that you can travel a few miles and find people speaking in completely different accents. It's not just a tonal difference. They'll emphasize different sounds, use different inflections at the end of sentences. The point is that for those living there it's all just accepted, it's not thought peculiar and it's automatically picked up by children. Only a visitor notices the differences.

It's the same in Christian circles. We have our own definitions and emphases, often the result of years of accepted use.

Take the word 'missionary'. This word carries with it notions of sacrifice and significance that set them apart from the ordinary run-of-the-mill employment contexts. For most Christians, 'missionaries' are people who work overseas. They may actually not be working as pastors or itinerant evangelists, instead working in schools, hospitals or businesses, but because they are abroad, they are seen as special and so need special support from the whole church. They are heroes.

However, those who work in the same contexts in this country are often seen as simply engaged in a job and won't be prayed for by the whole church; after all, they aren't understood to be missionaries. But isn't every Christian called to mission? And is it easier or harder to show and share the gospel in a Nairobi business than in a Newcastle factory? We have to stop using the language of 'full-time Christian work' when we actually mean 'paid Christian employment'.

Another example would be 'disciple' – for some it only refers to 'keen' Christians rather than carrying notions of what being a normal Christian is all about. It's not the words alone that matter; it's also the way the words are used and understood – it's our local dialect that actually determines its real meaning.

Our use of language can reveal who our heroes are – the people and causes that receive most of the gathered church's attention. They may be celebrated in story, 'rewarded' with specific prayerful attention and valued by the whole congregation. For example, the church youth leader may be the hero, while the teacher is just doing an 'ordinary' job, and the Christian pupil may be forgotten about altogether. You can tell a lot about a culture of a church by noticing who its heroes are. And you can begin to change the culture of a church by shining the spotlight on new heroes.

There is nothing wrong with supporting one another, nor honouring people in difficult situations. But there is something wrong if our symbols reveal that we only consider some people, in some situations, as worthy of such support.

The beliefs we share
The most powerful aspects of church culture are the deep beliefs and assumptions that are held by the majority of

people that shape their actions and words. These deep beliefs may be spoken, but often aren't. They are simply assumed, and built on. So, for example, it is often assumed that overseas missionaries are engaged in a more significant work than Christians employed in the local supermarket. These beliefs provide most of the emotional energy that protects the status quo.

Our accepted behaviour ('the way we do things round here') and the symbols ('These things are important to us') flow directly from our core beliefs and assumptions. This is why it is so important that churches have a rigorous theology that will undergird whole-life disciple-making. Stories, heroes and actions all emerge from our deepest beliefs.

So imagine you're a church leader – if you aren't one already. Two sixteen-year-old boys go to a Christian festival and come back with stories to share. One says that he feels sure that God wants him to go to Bible college in a few years to set out upon the road to ordained ministry. He has gifts that suggest he might be right to think that.

The other comes back saying that he feels God wants him to continue developing his football skills. He's been spotted by the local professional team and he's there as an apprentice. He has gifts that suggest he might be right to think that.

What would you do for the first boy? What would you encourage him to read? Would you meet with him regularly? What would you begin to ask him to do? How would you mentor him? What would you warn him about?

What about the second boy? What would you do for him?

Now imagine you're a member of that church – which of the two boys would you be praying for, going up to congratulate, cheering on?

What might your answers suggest about the culture of your church, about what you believe to be important, about your view of God and his mission, about what the 'good' Christian life might look like?

When I was a vice principal in a Bible college I had a conversation with a student who was just about to graduate. 'So what are you going to do?' I asked. 'I don't know, but I don't want to go back into secular work,' the student replied. 'Why not?' 'Because I really want to serve God,' was the answer.

Where had the student picked up the idea that you could only 'really serve God' if you were working for a Christian organization? The college had not explicitly taught him this way of looking at the world, and yet it ran deep within his belief system and, at that time, the college's deepest belief system, even though neither I nor anyone else on the staff would have advocated it.

It happened because the people who were invited to speak at college worship gatherings were church leaders or para-church workers with exciting tales of life on their church-centred frontlines. It happened because the best college lecturers became the college heroes. But it began long before college life began for the student.

Many of them were given special attention before they left to join the college. They were invited to share how they came to be aware of their 'call'. Although they had not yet been trained, they may have been encouraged to preach. People might have given them financial help so that they could study debt-free. They certainly were prayed for by the whole congregation on their last Sunday before the course began. And when they went back for holidays, people were interested to know what they had been learning. All of this is great. Students need support. But *all* students need support: those studying subjects such as English, mathematics or sports science, not just those going to study in a Christian context.

Therefore, it was not surprising to see how students reacted to their pre-college life: that's what they left behind. Compared to their excitement about what lay in front of them – for most, a new career in the 'Christian world' – the past looked drab.

It was a deeply embedded culture, unspoken and therefore mostly unexamined.

In the case of this individual student, the danger is that if he found employment in Christian circles, he would, unwittingly, perpetuate this sacred–secular divided culture in whatever organization or church he joined. It would be a spiritual disaster. And if he didn't find employment in a 'Christian' organization, he would feel as if he was wasting his life. And that too would be a spiritual disaster.

It's these unspoken beliefs that result in the old mantra being played out time after time in workplaces, societies and churches across the world: 'Culture eats strategy for breakfast.' In other words, you can have a sparkling new whole-life mission strategy for your church that everyone thinks is a grand idea, but unless you address the underlying beliefs, unless you start honouring new types of hero, new ways of being missional, then the existing culture will have consigned your sparkling new strategy to oblivion before it gets going. You'll be planting acorns in sand.

If you pursue new goals without recognizing that your organization is very likely to be operating in a way designed to deliver the old goals, then it is highly unlikely you will achieve those goals. Don't expect to hear lots of stories about fruitfulness in the workplace if the prayer bulletins are only about overseas world mission. This vital truth explains why so many attempts to change fail. If the central beliefs are not challenged and changed, if the activities that define us are not adapted and if there are no changes in the signs and symbols around us, then no amount of new strategic thinking will lead to change.

You'll always fail to change the central culture of a church if you think it'll be enough to add a 'God at work' group, alongside the home groups, men's groups or the photography club. You may well feel that people can be helped if they choose to opt into the group, but fundamentally the rest of church life will not change. In fact, to introduce such a group may do more harm than good, because now people will say, 'Oh, we don't need to change, we already do that – we have a work group.'

Of course, there is a role for 'special interest' groups, but the reason the 'God at work' group sitting alongside all the other special interest groups may not be helpful is because it will suggest that thinking theologically and missionally about work is only for a particular group of people: the keen ones, the clever ones, the interested ones, the ones with time on their hands. And so only a few people might attend, even though a large number of people work. If, in your congregation, the majority of people are in paid work, then this focus needs to be core to the activities in church life. It needs to be reflected on in the sermons and in the 'ordinary' small groups that already exist.

And, of course, this is not just about paid work. Lots of people do volunteer work and many retired people need to understand why their work did matter, and they need to be envisioned to support people who are still at work, and to see the kingdom potential in what they do now. And for those who would hope to return to work, they need to be prepared for all that lies ahead of them.

Culture matters

In sum, if you don't take seriously the question of culture, then it is unlikely that you will see any long-term differences.

However, church cultures can change, and (in our experience) have done so, though often the changes will be slow. But if the new actions are authentic expressions of the whole-life missional values, then over time the church's culture will change. The evidence that they have changed may be quite small, but will exist.

In the early days, intentional actions to help a culture change will have to be persistent and may appear a little 'forced'. You may have to overemphasize one aspect of life at the expense of others in order to establish a culture shift. But keep going: change can happen and the prize of a whole-life disciple-making church is worth chasing.

Imagine has made me totally rethink my 'frontline'. I ask every day, 'God, what have I done to bring glory to you today?' And I ask him to give me the 'tools' to do the job. It's made me realize that, instead of trying to be the 'best mum' and the 'best wife' first, if I try to be the *best disciple* first then that will make me a better wife, mother, friend, colleague, daughter, sister, auntie . . .

And the church has begun to realize 'the call to worship' is not 10.40 am on a Sunday morning but every day when we open our eyes until we shut them to sleep.
Member, Imagine Pilot Church

Among the church members, I've noticed a passion for living the life that God has planned for us and a need to share that in all aspects of life. I've noticed people being apprehensive about going about that, but wanting to do it anyway, wanting to help each other with life and faith.
Church leader, Imagine Pilot Church

Pause for thought

1. In one church that worked with us on the pilot project, the members identified what attracted the church's 'column inches and air-time minutes'. In other words, what gets talked about a lot and what is written about in church notices indicates what is deemed to be significant. What would your 'air-time minutes and column inches' say about what is important in your church?
2. What advice would you have given to those two boys returning from the summer camp?
3. How has the culture of your church changed over the years? How has it happened? What has the church learned from these experiences about how to introduce change successfully?

Further reading

Collins, Jim, *Good to Great in the Social Sector* (Random House, 2006).
Greene, Mark, *The Great Divide* (LICC, 2010).
Kotter, John, *Leading Change* (Harvard Business Press, 1996).
Marshall, Colin and Payne, Tony, *The Trellis and the Vine* (Matthias Press, 2009).
The Alban Institute: www.alban.org

*There is the tension between the need for an easy
discipleship process through which we can
efficiently herd lots of people and the patient,
plodding and ultimately mysterious nature
of the spiritual transformation process.*

Ruth Haley Barton,
Strengthening the Soul of your Leadership

How to become a whole-life disciple-making church

Things have to change. Once we become convinced of the need to change, we can never believe that we can continue as we have done in the past, where church-sponsored mission receives all our attention and the bulk of our everyday life is overlooked.

So how can that change happen? If you're an activist, this is the chapter that you wanted at the beginning of the book. But the danger of racing to the concrete actions that produce change is that we might well have overlooked the fundamental shift that needs to take place in the culture of church. So, for the sake of clarity, let us revisit the fundamental principles that need to be present for whole-life disciple-making churches to develop, before outlining the process that appears to lead to lasting change.

Fundamental principles guiding a whole-life disciple-making church

The goal of a whole-life disciple-making church arises from the biblical conviction that Jesus is Lord of all and that the core vocation of the church is to make whole-life missionary disciples. As we have said, it's easy for this to be assumed and thereby overlooked. It's critical that people can see the direct connection between our worship of Jesus as Lord and the way we live our everyday lives. If this is made explicit, then the proposed changes will not be easily dismissed as this season's concern.

It is on this basis of the Lordship of Christ and the vocation of the church that a church can be invited to develop a whole-life culture so that whole-life missionary discipleship becomes central and fruitful for all. The call to live as agents of the kingdom of God is extended to everyone. Regardless of age, social standing, Christian experience, temperament or any other differences, all who surrender to the claims of Christ are called to live fruitfully for God's sake. The promise of John 15 is not only that it is God's intention that disciples do live fruitful lives, but that it will be this fruit that provides the evidence that you are indeed a disciple (John 15:8).

This expectation of fruitfulness calls for a shift in our understanding about the church. We need to see that the church has a whole-life mission, and that this mission takes place when the church is gathered and scattered. Both matter. In order for this mission to bear fruit, we need to help one another to grow in Christian maturity, a maturity that is not simply in understanding but that gives new ways of addressing the common challenges of life.

The Bible talks about this growth being 'in the grace and knowledge of our Lord and Saviour' (2 Peter 3:18). This conclusion to Peter's second epistle reflects his introductory section. In the light of the divine power which gives us all we need 'for life and godliness', he urges his readers to add to their faith goodness, knowledge, self-control, perseverance, godliness, brotherly kindness and love (2 Peter 1:3–7). As these qualities become part of our natural lives, 'they will keep [us] from being ineffective and unproductive in [our] knowledge of our Lord Jesus Christ' (2 Peter 1:8). All these qualities are tested in the realities of everyday life. It's here that we will make sure that our knowledge of Jesus will not have been in vain.

The process of becoming a whole-life disciple-making church

As the implications of these principles are explored, then the process of change begins. Because it's a process, and because churches are about people, not industrial units, the process is never a smooth, linear process. People leave, people join, people face crises, people get tired. The aim is not to become intolerant about the realities of life. It's to ensure that the intention of the church is to become a whole-life disciple-making community. It takes time for this perspective to be natural, but once it is, it affects people's prayers, our worship together, our preaching, our conversations in small groups, our expectations of fruitfulness – everything.

Fundamental to this is the recognition that what is being described here is the starting point for a journey towards whole-life disciple-making, not its final destination. It may be that we will never feel that we have reached a final destination, since every church experiences new Christians joining the church who need to grasp the full implications of life in the kingdom of God and more experienced Christians moving into the fellowship who may find the emphasis to be a new one. Every generation needs to keep on experiencing renewal of the vision, and the freedom to experiment with changes that make most sense at that point of their story together. Therefore, it seems better to outline the change process as a circular action, one where you keep on revisiting and reinforcing changes that have been made earlier, as follows.

1. Cast a vision

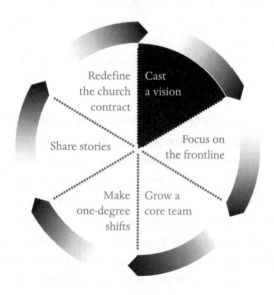

It's essential that people in church know what the vision is – because it is going to have profound implications for them. This is a vision that has far more direct effects on every member of the church than recruiting a new member of staff, or opening a church-linked café, or extending the building, or even planting a new congregation. All of these things can be done and, to varying degrees, can leave individual members unaffected. But once the church family have accepted the challenge of equipping every follower of Jesus to live as whole-life disciples, everyone is included.

For some leaders, even the mention of the word 'vision' is enough to provoke groaning and sighing that words cannot express. There has been so much emphasis on vision in recent years. Indeed, for many of us in leadership, the question, 'So what's your vision for the church?' fills us with unease, as though it's ours alone and we are the sole guardian of it. What the question normally boils down to is: 'What are you going to do about "ABC" [attendance, buildings, cash]?' In other words, the request for a vision is all about our life as gathered church.

What we are calling for here is a response to the vision question that simply says, our vision is that we will live our whole lives for the glory of God and we will equip one another to do that faithfully and well, prompting us to live in such a way when it seems as though we have forgotten how to do so. We will be a disciple-making missionary church.

Those asking the question may still want to know about ABC, but at least they'll know your vision includes D – disciples.

This has to happen through people being able to see how this is rooted in the gospel and demonstrated over and over throughout Scripture. It's easy for the gospel to be heard as though it is simply a 'rescue' package, rather than as a recruitment for a new cause. A cause with a new Lord, a new mission and a new hope, only made possible through salvation.

How you cast this vision will depend on your own situation. At LICC, we have developed a range of resources that might help you do this.[1] The resources will help shape weekends away, day courses, sermon series, small groups and leadership teams to grapple with the main issues. But, whatever resources are used, there needs to be at least one person who is so passionately committed to seeing whole-life discipleship become a reality that they will not give up on the cause. But the vision is also caught when people have the chance to share their existing experiences and are then encouraged to see something different.

Sharing our experiences: a whole-life survey[2]

For the vision to be earthed, people need to understand how it interacts with their everyday lives. We have found that using a survey is a really effective way of enabling this to begin to happen.

We developed a survey for completion by, and sharing with, the whole congregation. It helps the congregation explore the basic question: 'Where are we as a church in relation to whole-life discipling and mission?' This is not a general survey about the health of the church or the effectiveness of the programmes, nor is it an evaluation of the church team's performance. It is asking the question, 'Where is our Christian life being lived out and what is enabling us to live fruitfully?'

The survey has three main outcomes:

1. It provides an opportunity to hear about people's experiences on life's frontlines, the opportunities and challenges they present for people's discipleship.
2. It provides a snapshot of where the church currently is by allowing church members the opportunity to provide honest feedback about their impressions and perceptions of the church community and how it equips them for life on the frontline.
3. It provides the means of creating a new conversation in the congregation.

The very act of asking the questions begins the process of changing a culture. However, the real value of the survey is not the numerical results, which reflect relative strengths and weaknesses – the real value is that it enables people to begin to talk to one another about the whole-life vision. This enables everyone to recognize that these are serious issues, and creates an expectation that we will all grow, develop and discover how God might be able to use us where we are.

The feedback is probably most easily given at a time when relaxed conversation can take place. Indeed, we have found that sharing and discussing the results with the whole congregation can become a wonderful occasion to reinforce the vision and begin to generate unity of purpose and new ideas.

On the whole, our experience is that people do care about their church. They want to belong to a community that is making a clear difference in their own lives. And many of these people have clear ideas about what changes could be implemented that would bring a new sense of purpose and vision for the congregation as disciples.

This commitment to a process of change takes courage, creativity and determination. It's necessary to hear the truth about the present situation, and recognize a reasonable response, rather than merely reacting from a defensive position. The use of the survey provides this opportunity.

One of the churches on the pilot project was an English-speaking Chinese church. Over the years it had been the church that had welcomed, cared for and sustained students from the Far East during their studies at university. Some of them stayed in the area after graduation; others moved on all around the world. However, the church recognized that church life had changed over the forty years of their existence. Students were coming to the city from Singapore, Hong Kong and Malaysia having experienced international churches in their home countries. They were at home in Western worship settings, and no longer automatically looked for a spiritual home that was more culture-specific.

The church leaders recognized that they had a responsibility to equip their members to reach out in mission to the British-born people they were working with, rather than just concentrating on the next generation of students. They wanted to concentrate on equipping people for their workplaces in particular, but they struggled to enthuse the younger members of their congregation about this. Doing the survey highlighted the reason for the struggle they were having. People were strung out with church events.

If you had seen their gathered church programme you would have understood. It was really crowded – worship events, teaching events, Chinese language classes, children's and youth work, fellowship events, inter-church events, evangelistic events. There really was little room for the most committed members of the church to socialize with anyone else, let alone give attention to issues outside their gathered church life.

After they did the survey together, they decided that one way they could help people gain a new perspective on the gathered-scattered church was to meet only on Sunday mornings during August. All the other meetings were cancelled. That gave people the time to reflect on how they were living as missionary disciples among their colleagues and friends. It was a way of helping them see what life could be like without so many gathered church events, and therefore to see which activities they should then restart to help them be fruitful in all of life.

This may not seem a big deal to anyone not involved in that particular church. Indeed, it might feel normal. But for them it was deeply countercultural. They tend to feel the pressure of their own cultural background that drives them to keep working, that makes them feel guilty if they slacken the pace.

The leaders recognized that if they challenged an unhealthy aspect of their own Chinese culture and enabled people to retreat from a packed agenda of gathered church activities, they would signal a shift in what 'good Christian living looked like'.

> The effect was that people were surprised but delighted to have the space and time that they were not expecting. It also served as a strong symbol that for them being a Christian was not simply a matter of being engaged in gathered church activities. They were signalling that they were aware of the new frontlines that they wanted people to see more clearly.

Cancelling a few meetings would be no big deal for many of us, but for them the message was loud and clear. And when they went back to continuing their fuller programme in September, they did so recognizing the relationship between their gathered activities and their scattered lives.

The task of enabling change to take place is crucial. In one sense, if everyone has grasped a renewed vision of the Lordship of Christ, has understood the implications of that for their frontline and has been able to share their stories of everyday life, it will be clear that changes are necessary so that everyone can flourish. However well people may feel that their church community is doing at supporting one another, it is inevitable that more could happen.

Seeing something different

We have found that some people have been envisioned through the written word: the essay and DVD *Imagine* or *The Great Divide* produced by LICC over the years have led to a light-bulb moment for many. It's not so much that it was a new vision; rather the ideas were presented in ways that articulated what they had intuitively been feeling.

Others have benefited from teaching on a church weekend away, when they have been able to think through all that is being said in a relaxed way. Some churches began the process of change by preaching a set of sermons around the issues people face at work. But after the series, they didn't think that they could tick that box and move on to other issues; they used it as a strategic beginning to help the church think through fruitfulness for everyone's frontlines.

Some church leadership groups have visited churches that have begun this journey so that they might begin really to believe that it is a possibility in their own places. For others it has happened far more spontaneously. One church leader went on holiday and worshipped in one of the churches we were working with, came home, reflected on what he had heard and what they were doing in his own church, then contacted us to see how they could take steps forward.

One of the churches brought all their older people to an envisioning day for church leaders. The pastor reckoned that if it was going to work in his church, he needed the older folks to be on board with it all. The speaker at the vision day found it a bit of a challenge and a surprise to have fifteen people in their early seventies in the seminar, but everyone coped. The older folk got it (and why wouldn't they?), and the church was able to begin the change process.

Maybe the range of possibilities should not be surprising if we dare to believe that the Spirit of God is involved in this work. The crucial thing is that people have a chance to realize all that might be possible and are encouraged that they could experience real fruitfulness as they live faithfully on their frontlines.

2. Focus on the frontline

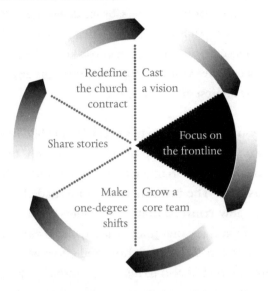

The work of connecting the life of the gathered church to the frontline begins by listening. This listening will lead to understanding. But its primary motivation should be a desire to affirm the frontline as a place of significance. Listening is one of the things that we all know we could be better at, so we are unsurprised when we are encouraged to do it more, but surprised when we see the consequences of taking people's situations seriously. If we want people to approach their frontline with renewed imagination, we will have to practise the art of listening to one another.

One way leaders can 'listen' is to make the effort to visit people on their frontlines. And it can prove to be incredibly powerful on a number of levels:

A new vicar decided to visit his church warden's workplace. The warden was the founder and managing director of this business. Suddenly, as they were walking around the factory that he had built, this fifty-year-old man, who had served in the church for over twenty years, broke down and began to weep. The vicar put his arm round him and asked, 'What's wrong?' The entrepreneur said, 'Do you know I've been in the church twenty-five years and this is the first time anyone has shown any interest in what I do here.'

For twenty-five years, this man's everyday life had been of no significance to the leadership of his local church, the church he loved and had given so much to. He wasn't bitter about this, but he was hurt. The investment of time made by the vicar opened up new conversations, a broader awareness of the reality of life and for one man at least, the reassurance that the business that took so much time and effort was important – not only to God but also to his local church community.

If the church is going to be successful at linking its gathered life with its life as scattered disciples, listening will not just be an exercise in affirmation; it will also be an intentional occasion for learning. It will provide the material that provokes preachers to think through their sermons. It will provoke new conversations in small groups. It will enable the church members to know whether their ministry to one another is bearing fruit.

Stories are going to be the main currency in a whole-life disciple-making church. Stories of the challenges and the fruitfulness of people's lives will reveal the extent to which we are equipping people to live as missionary disciples. Therefore, there has to be a determined attempt to take the time to listen to people's experiences. Leaders need to be among a number of story-gatherers. These story-gatherers need to be able to listen for the significance of what people are experiencing, learn from their experiences and reflect together on what it all means.

3. Grow a core team

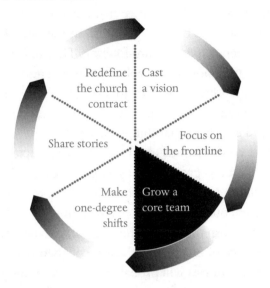

The Imagine process is about the church working together to equip one another, so it is important that the process doesn't stay as a clergy-driven initiative. It's easy for leaders to be overwhelmed by the range of issues with which they need to engage. And it's easy for the process to stay in the area of 'good intentions'. A core team of 'champions', whose sole focus is enabling their church to become a whole-life disciple-making community, ensures that a church can take strides forward on the whole-life agenda.

Our experience is that when we have asked churches to appoint a core team, each has had a different composition. Some were made up of existing leaders, some had a group of people not in formal leadership, while others were mixed. Some groups were large, others really small. Some had authority to act directly; others could only suggest changes. What they all had in common was a determination not to let the changes that were necessary stay as merely good intentions.

You need to gather people into this group who are convinced of the significance of the change that needs to happen. They may be people who have been critical in the past about the church's tendency to be inward-looking. They may have been people who have not been involved in many church committees or groups, precisely because they have seen the significance of serving God in wider society. These people need to be encouraged to believe that things can change.

The first conversations about whole-life discipleship have to be had with this group. If they cannot see how this would make a difference for them in their own lives, they will never be able to encourage anyone else to embrace it. They not only have to grasp the vision; they also have to be gripped by the importance of change for the sake of their own discipleship. Your first stories will probably come from this group.

As long as the team of people is not overbalanced with paid church workers or people who are able to volunteer a lot of hours to the church, this team will also be made up of people who are balancing out the demands of the 10-110. Their responses will, it is hoped, be realistically applicable to their own lives. If it doesn't work for them, it's not going to work for anyone else.

Only then can they begin to oversee the envisioning process with others. They need to decide the best process for communicating the vision to the whole church. The teams we worked with would normally meet every four to six weeks. Ask them to make a commitment to the group for twelve months. It makes it manageable for people, gives them a 'get out' moment, but also should focus your thinking together. The process of change will take longer than a year – in our experience it is nearer three to four years, so it will be good to have different people ensuring that the process doesn't stall.

As well as ensuring that the process keeps progressing, they are the group that keeps everyone accountable to the process. Leaders can easily encourage people to imagine new possibilities, but then lose confidence, or get distracted, or read another book, or attend another conference. The best core groups keep everyone focused on the task.

4. Make one-degree shifts

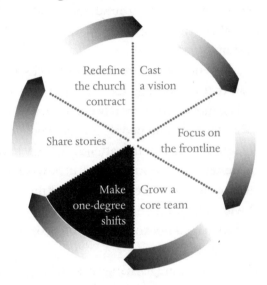

The danger of embracing the need for change is to imagine that everything needs to change all at once. The vision of a whole-life disciple-making church is a big vision. But the process of transitioning to such a church can be made by taking 'one-degree shifts'. This is an image taken from a compass. If you are walking in one direction and then make a single degree shift, eventually, if you walk far enough, you will end up in a very different place. The change will be imperceptible at first, but time will highlight its significance.

We have many examples of these small changes. These changes can be introduced by leaders, suggested by the congregation or, in some cases, led by individuals in the congregation. One businesswoman was convinced of the need to create whole-life disciples but was part of a busy church. Undaunted, she began a 'whole-life prayer meeting' once a month to highlight the issues people were facing on their frontlines. After eight months, around seventy-five to eighty people now meet to pray around these issues. And it's beginning to affect the perspective of the whole church. A one-degree shift.

However, depending on the circumstances facing the church, it can require courage for a team of core leaders to take action. The move – from merely being pleased with a full church to wanting to equip people for the whole of life – is occasionally unwanted by church attendees. They have joined the church under one 'contract' and it now seems to be changing. It takes skill to address this. Most of the leaders who were faced with this situation introduced change slowly and carefully, and managed not to alienate the people they were attempting to win to the cause.

The decision to encourage change in small degrees is taken knowingly. Of course, it is obvious that once this process of incremental change begins, other elements of church life will also be affected. But it allows cautious leaders to accept that they can be part of a change process. It also means that changes can be introduced that will not lead to major church rows. The downside of this approach is that none of the changes look particularly daring to anyone outside that particular context. But this is the point. They are not meant to be spectacular transformations, merely part of a long-term process that will lead to a more profound shift in emphasis. The changes are ones that will be relevant to the particular tradition of that particular church. You don't need to do what everybody else is doing; you do what is helpful for your particular church family, at this time, in this place. The changes that have the greatest effect are those which are suggested by the local church. It may be that their ideas are not original. They may have discovered them along the way, but because they feel that they are relevant to their local context, they are more likely to pursue them relentlessly.

These changes need to be able to carry the DNA of the new culture that is envisaged. So each small change should be clearly focused on the larger task of transforming the culture of the local church. A simple way of finding out whether a proposed change will function in this way is to ask, 'How will this help us to become more of a whole-life disciple-making church?' If it's not clear how this will happen, the changes may be desirable and even welcomed, but they are not in line with the overall task.

For example, you may decide that the church needs to decorate its entrance foyer in a more contemporary style. Obviously this is generally a good idea if it means you can clear out the dog-eared notices, repaint walls and fix new signs. But if that's all that is intended, the decision is not focused enough on the task in hand. The need for decoration offers an opportunity to think about the foyer's function as a bridge between the world of corporate worship and scattered lives of mission. So as well as the general renovation, thought should be given to the pictures put up on the walls. What messages could help people see the link between all that is going to happen in the building, and the rest of life? For example, would it be possible to get someone to take some good photographs of church members in their workplaces and display them in the foyer? They could have some biblical texts included about serving God in 'word and deed', or they may be powerful enough without the need for a text. Either way, they would make a welcome change from the more 'sacred' images we are used to.

The danger with one-degree shifts is that it can seem as though there is a lack of urgency about all that needs to be different. If the small changes are not viewed against the larger intentions, then the changes will remain small. However, if they are seen as levers that enable the beginning of a broader change in culture, then they can be very effective.

This Time Tomorrow (TTT)

'TTT' is an idea that has been around for a long time, but when local churches hear about it they are keen to introduce it, and this small inclusion into a service always repays the effort taken.

'TTT' stands for 'This Time Tomorrow'. This is a simple way of enabling someone to be given the opportunity to be interviewed for three or four minutes, answering three questions such as the following, and then being prayed for.

1. What will you be doing this time tomorrow?
2. What opportunities or challenges will you face?
3. How can we pray for you?

Of course, this can seem superficial or inadequate, only skimming the surface of anyone's true life. But its significance lies on a number of different levels:

- It emphasizes that all of life does matter to God and to the congregation.
- It encourages people to recognize the significance of their 'ordinary places'.
- It acknowledges, affirms and honours the person being interviewed.

- It encourages people to pray for one another.
- It signals to everyone that our gathered worship is connected with our daily lives.
- It creates the possibility of new conversations around the issues that take up most of our emotional energies.
- It can mark the beginning of the dismantling of the sacred–secular divide.[3]

TTT is a moment that can be a mark of solidarity in the congregation. If you have been interviewing someone in one of the service industries, you could invite everyone else who is in a similar context to stand, or put their hands up, or, in a shy church, wink to indicate that they would like to be included in the prayer.

The asking of these questions, and others like them, can become the means whereby we encourage one another to grow as whole-life disciples. Engaging with these questions begins to allow a new culture to emerge in the local church. The activities of the gathered church are no longer seen to be the only significant ones. The whole of life is being recognized and valued.

Other examples of one-degree shifts

Along with some of the ideas we have already outlined, one-degree shifts have been introduced into different areas of a church's life together.

In the worship services

Here, they have included the following:

- Preachers intentionally changing their focus of sermon application. This may seem obvious, but some preachers have been provoked into thinking about the situations facing the people in the congregation and how the sermons can be of most help. Some preachers might feel this is pandering to 'felt needs' rather than enabling people to wrestle with Scripture. It could be seen as that, until you remember that the fundamental nature of the gathering is that of whole-life missionaries who come together with experiences of living out the implications of the gospel in their various areas of life through the week. Preachers need to listen to these experiences to know how best to equip people. The response may well be through a range of approaches to Scripture: expositional preaching, or reflections on core doctrines. What is important is that the purpose will be the equipping of these missionary disciples.

- Worship leaders have thought about the songs that are sung, taking care to avoid ones that have a strong sacred–secular bias.

- Those leading prayers have been encouraged to find the stories of the scattered church to weave into their intercessions.

- People have been encouraged to share frontline testimonies, stories of how they have been used by God to be a means of blessing in their everyday lives. This is also a vital way of building on TTT – otherwise there is the danger of simply sharing solidarity in people's challenge rather than building hope and confidence through the testimonies of what God has been doing. Churches have projected quotes on screens that encourage people to think about the issues that shape their lives as they prepare for worship, so at dedication services or christenings, there may be a set of quotes with images to help the congregation think about the challenge of raising children; a series at Lent could include quotes about greed or generosity. They have wanted to connect the 'religious' activity that is about to begin with the everyday challenge of living faith out in the different contexts in which we find ourselves.

- Others have used rolling slides of the front pages of the Sunday newspapers amid encouragements to pray.
- One church put a mirror on the church missionary noticeboard. Every time people looked at the news from overseas missionaries, they couldn't avoid seeing their own face reflected back. The message was clear: they too were missionaries.

All of these changes may be small, but all reinforce the message that we are in a place that takes discipling for the sake of the world seriously.

In small groups

Small groups are a feature of the life of many churches. They are an obvious place where the formation of whole-life disciples can take centre stage.

- One church encouraged their groups to take a number of weeks to get to know each other really well, by asking questions of each other about their everyday lives, praying for them and encouraging each other to have a sense of how God might be able to use them. In smaller groups, it's easier to spend more time together thinking through our situations in depth. These questions could be used as a basis for a group to think through the issues together:
  - Describe how you spend an 'ordinary' day.
  - What is the impact of these activities on your health, on your family?
  - What do you find most satisfying about your normal activities?
  - What causes you the greatest stress?

> – How does being a Christian make a difference to you?
> – How does your faith connect with your work/the
>   primary way you spend your time?[4]

- One church changed the format of small groups,
  encouraging them to meet in smaller numbers than
  they had been used to, and used new resources that
  allowed them to address real-life issues.
- Although some people have used prayer triplets in the
  past and struggled to keep them going, many are now
  realizing the benefit of a prayer triplet in enabling
  accountability and perseverance.
- Churches began to open up their leadership training to
  those who were leaders in areas of life other than church
  life. Others, who were training preachers, realized that
  their teaching on communication skills would be helpful
  to a much wider group than just lay preachers.

In one-on-one relationships

- Some churches have introduced mentoring schemes
  partnering younger people with older Christians. The
  emphasis has been on life lived in the contexts of new
  relationships, or changes in life, or the reality of starting
  on new career paths.
- Because one church wanted to encourage people to
  continue their discussions over coffee, they had simple
  discussion questions on the tables that people could
  engage with if they chose to do so.

In communications

- One church realized that they needed to have more
  stories of what God was doing with people in everyday

life, and they appointed 'in-house journalists' to find those stories, write them up and share them with the wider church.

- Another church has taken their TTT interviews and put them on their website. Anyone who is searching for a church in that area of the country is in no doubt as to what matters to the church.
- One church included the question 'How are we doing at making disciples?' on the agenda of every PCC meeting.
- One church included a column on the church address list to include the places where people worked.

These are small things. It doesn't take much effort to add a column to the church address list to include a workplace, but it's a huge symbol that our life together as gathered church is about a much wider horizon than simply what happens in the church building. Can you imagine the conversations that ripple out – 'Did you know . . . ?', 'I didn't realize our church was doing that . . . ' and so on.

Although most of our work so far has been with individual churches, we have also worked with clusters of churches that all belong to the same denomination or are in the same geographical area. One such cluster was in Milton Keynes. After a period of working with the leadership groups, envisioning, explaining and provoking ideas, they decided that one of the responses they could make was to work together on specific issues. So on one Sunday morning, while the rest of the churches were worshipping in their own buildings, they invited all those involved in education to come together and reflect on their mission as Christian educationalists, realize who else was involved in teaching and be prayed for. Ideally, they could have included the church youth workers and children's workers in the conversations as well. They intend to continue this over time with the different groups of people that are represented in their churches. For many, this may seem a lot more than a one-degree shift.

Some of the responses that churches have made together may appear to be obvious or too small to be worthy of comment. However, the point of a one-degree shift is that it is not for anyone else to comment. They are relevant to their local context. The change was introduced in response to their situations, the changes were able to be implemented and they did make a difference there. And they led to further changes. The key is that each church identifies its own one-degree shifts. Only then will real, lasting change begin.

If culture, at its simplest, involves the 'way we do things round here' as mentioned earlier, then doing different 'things round here' alongside challenging some of the deeply held beliefs and assumptions about mission and disciple-making will, over time, establish a different culture.

5. Share stories

The danger of this process is that it can easily slip back into a church renewal programme alone. It has to be remembered that the goal of all this envisioning, listening and changing is not that we have a more fulfilling, or even more relevant, experience of church together. The purpose is that people might live fruitful disciple-reproducing lives when they are scattered throughout towns and cities in their everyday lives. Ultimately, the purpose is to show and share the gospel with our nation so that many might come to know Jesus.

So it is important that fruitfulness is celebrated. The final chapter will look at the signs of growth and change, but one of the crucial signs of fruitfulness will be the stories that are shared. In a world that is driven by productivity targets, to rely on stories can seem inadequate. But we need to remember the work we are involved in. The goal of a church community is to glorify God. This is not measurable by size, perceived significance or national exposure. We glorify God as we bear fruit for him (John 15). And because most of us spend our lives in relatively small circles, this fruit will be borne there.

So how will we measure whether our emphasis on whole-life discipleship has made any difference? We will know through the conversations that we have with Christians as we hear their increasing awareness of all that God has called them to be and to do. We will know because we will hear about people living out the good news of God intentionally so that others around them can be let in on it. We will know because we will hear of people who have committed their lives to following Jesus. We will know because we will hear of people who have enabled situations to change to reflect the values of the kingdom of God, encouraging justice, mercy and love.

We have seen that in churches where these changes have been made, there is an increase in the number of such stories to be heard. At first the stories may be small stories, but someone needs to listen well and to find the significance of the stories. Most of the stories that I've retold here were not seen to be significant by the people involved. They were just getting on with their lives. But once they had been able to see a reaction to what they had lived through that affirmed, encouraged and valued them, they were encouraged to continue to grow.

This dignifying of people's stories is vital redeeming work. It takes the ordinary and suggests that God might be able to do something extraordinary with it. It liberates people to see their own lives differently and encourages others to be equally creative.

I met a young father whose wife is in a wheelchair. His 'work' is to be his wife's carer. She's suffering from MS. They were people in a similar position to many others, feeling that the situation they were in was a difficult one, one where they would not thrive, one where it is easy to believe that they could not be used by God.

But they didn't let this situation define them. As we were chatting he told me that when they moved into their present house, they decided to knock on each of the doors in their avenue to introduce themselves. As he put it, 'We can't go very far because of our circumstances, so we need to make sure that we are able to know the people around us.'

They had a purpose behind this. They wanted to build relationships with their neighbours so that they would be able to invite them round for barbecues in the summer and drinks in the winter. They wanted to be able to share their faith, even in the midst of their difficulties.

One of the neighbours told them that they were the first people who had ever introduced themselves like this before on the avenue. Over the next months, it became a lot easier to invite their neighbours round, because they had taken the first move of introducing themselves.

Here is a couple whose world has become very small. One might have excused them for thinking that they didn't have frontlines any longer. They created one for themselves.

This is just another small story of two people living fruitfully on their frontline, creating a different culture, enabling their Christian faith and hope to become visible to people around them.

There must be many stories like these. Once we grow used to looking for them, we can encourage one another to continue faithfully looking for ways to bless others around us.

6. Redefine the church contract

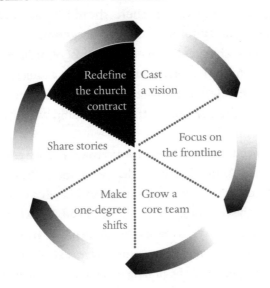

This is the final element of the change process. It's about the expectations that people have of the church. It also involves the understanding that those in paid church ministry have of their own roles. It's a big issue – so much so that it's dealt with at length in the next chapter.

The process of change is relatively easy to explain, but it's important to remember that for a culture to shift so that all of this becomes natural will take a longer period of time than we might wish.

At first changes may feel artificial. In time, the culture will shift so that it will all appear to be just what we do 'round here'. The crucial thing is that the core team of champions that have come together along with the leadership team remain committed and determined to see people enjoying the fruitfulness of life in the whole of their lives. The challenge is to keep everyone's focus on the central purpose when there are competing claims on the church's time and energy. The reality is that there will be times when it feels as though nothing has changed. But there should be an underlying conviction that cannot be dismissed or ignored.

All of these changes happen in the midst of ordinary church life. But for that to happen, there needs to be a radical renegotiation of the relationship between church leaders and the members of the church. It's this relationship we turn to next.

Nicky spends six months each year in Sierra Leone as a missionary. As the church has changed its focus, she has noticed that the church is increasingly supporting her as a whole person whether she is working in the UK or abroad. But what is also interesting, she says, is that as church members are coming to see themselves as missionaries themselves in their ordinary, daily lives, people are beginning to own what is happening abroad more as an extension of their ministry. It's not just what I'm doing but what we are doing a lot more.
Member, Imagine Pilot Church

What has changed as a pastor? 'The burden of being God, pressure to perform and get end results. Now you are more of

a signpost to God, a friend. Most important thing is not getting healed, but your relationship with God now – in their marriage, etc. It is more difficult but more releasing, less burdensome.'
Leader, Imagine Pilot Church

Pause for thought

1. Who could you meet to listen to their experiences on their frontline?
2. With whom do you share your stories? If you find it difficult to do so, why? What would help?
3. Who needs to hear about this vision in order for it to become a reality in your church?
4. What one-degree shifts can you imagine working in your church?

Further reading

Chester, Tim and Timmis, Steve, *Total Church* (Inter-Varsity Press, 2007).

Cotter, John, *A Sense of Urgency* (Harvard Business Press, 2008).

Crabtree, Davida, *The Empowering Church: How One Congregation Supports Lay People's Ministry in the World* (Alban, 1989).

Diehl, William, *Ministry in Daily Life* (Alban, 1996).

The Centered Life: www.centeredlife.org

When Jesus uses the word 'kingdom', and he uses it repeatedly and prominently, he is speaking in the largest and most comprehensive of terms. Nothing we do or feel or say is excluded from 'kingdom'. And if this is God's Kingdom, which it most certainly is, it means that everything that goes on is under God's rule, is penetrated by God's rule, is judged by God's rule, is included in God's rule – every one of my personal thoughts and feelings and actions, yes; but also the stock market in New York, the famine in the Sudan, your first grandchild born last night in Cambridge, the poverty in Calcutta, the suicide bombings in Tel Aviv and New York and Baghdad, the abortions in Dallas, the Wednesday night prayer meetings in Syracuse, the bank mergers being negotiated in London, Mexican migrants picking avocados in California – everything, absolutely everything, large and small: the kingdom of God in which Jesus is king.

Eugene Peterson,
The Jesus Way, pp. 202–203

All learning together:
redefining the church contract

In 1990, I was a young leader of an inner-city church that belonged to a denomination for whom mission was part of its core DNA. You didn't need to tell me that we needed to 'reach the UK', nor that we were called to 'make a difference where we were'. These phrases were second nature to us. The problem was that the 'we' only referred to us when we were involved in gathered church activities.

So everything revolved around the activities that ran from the church building. And believe me, that was a challenge. The church I inherited was 'quirky'. A congregation huddled behind steel-shuttered doors and barred windows, with barbed-wire protected roofs; it was a challenge to be engaged in mission when the primary strategy was to attract people to the church building. It didn't help that we had to bring in the security camera each week after the service, for fear that it would be stolen, or that we had to advise workmen to drive their vans into the church building so as not to have them taken from the car park.

However, we were not daunted. We engaged in gathered mission for all we were worth. And attract people we did – regular working-class people, people who taught in local schools or were social workers, teenagers who were part of the local neighbourhood gangs and one streaker who ran the length of the church during a candle-lit carol service. All of life was, indeed, there.

Why did anyone come? How did we grow? I have no idea. But I knew what my task was. I was the arrowhead of the church's mission activity. I was the recruiter for the vision. I was the heroic pathfinder of mission opportunities. I was the principal carer and teacher of the congregation.

And if things did not go as well as planned, I was ready to play the role of martyr ('Why can't things be different here?') or judge ('This church is hopeless').

At least in my mind.

So it was unsurprising that after seven years I was burned out, only fit to teach in Bible college while I rethought all that had happened to me, my understanding of the church and the role of ministry, and the challenge of mission. All of this is not to elicit sympathy; there are too many good stories to be told. The point is that the relationship I had with my church at that time was not dissimilar to many I see in other churches and other denominations with which I work. And it was a relationship that had not been written down on paper or even verbalized. In those days, it was unusual to get any sort of job description or indication of what was expected. We just tumbled into the situation for the very best of reasons. I wanted to lead a church that grew because people came to see the reality of salvation through Christ. The people in my church wanted to be a part of such a venture. We all just assumed that it would happen primarily through the activities of the gathered church with all the accompanying implications for the leader of that community. They had no expectation that I would be encouraging them to be missionary disciples in all of life. Nor did I. That wasn't part of the relationship

However, in all the churches that have begun to take seriously the call to become whole-life disciple-making communities, the most important change has been in the relationship between the leaders and the members of the church.

One of the most common reactions from leaders has been that they have had to make the biggest change in their thinking as leaders, in terms of their roles, the expectations that others had of them and the expectations they had of themselves. This is to be expected. When there is a renewed vision of the extent of the Lordship of Jesus and a renewed understanding of the relationship between the church in its gathered and scattered state, the understanding of the role of leadership will need to change.

If you assume that these changes can be introduced without any alteration in the role and activities of leadership, you haven't introduced a new vision, you've tweaked the existing vision, and you will end up in the same place.

This call for a changed understanding of the role of leaders needs to happen, because most leadership training is pre paring people for the existing culture of the church. In general terms, the training of church leaders happens in two ways:

1. They are either trained by the existing leaders of the local church, and so tend to reflect the existing culture of the church; or
2. They are trained in a college setting, away from their home environment, and so tend to reflect the existing culture of the college.

What both settings for training have in common is that they tend to assume the significance of the mission activities of the gathered church to the detriment of the scattered church. This assumption means that leadership is shaped in such a way that the leaders are unable or are too busy to understand how their ministry can equip people for the primary means of mission, individuals who live their life as scattered church.

For this to happen new skills are needed, new perspectives need to be encouraged, new actions engaged in and some unlearning of old habits and responses needs to be done. This chapter will reflect on the three changes that need to happen for churches to have a renewed relationship with their leaders:

1. a move from a pastoral *care* contract to a pastoral *equipping* contract;
2. a profound change in the psychology of the relationship between leaders and people; and
3. a broader focus by the leaders.

1. Moving from a pastoral *care* contract to a pastoral *equipping* contract

During a quarter of a century of being a church leader, I've known the joy of seeing people come to faith and join the church family, and the delight of Christians moving into the area, eager to be part of a local church. However, alongside these encouraging times, I've had the conversations with people that begin with the words, 'It's nothing personal, Neil, but . . . ' I always want to stop them and explain that if it's not personal, then I'm probably not the person they should be speaking to. But they seem to want to continue and outline all the issues that they see as problematic in the church and why they are going to leave. And as they draw to the end of their litany of complaint, if they really want to emphasize their unhappiness they will add, 'And above all, you don't care.'

And by that point they may be right.

But in twenty-five years I've not had someone come and say, 'And above all, you haven't helped me to live well for Christ as a disciple.' It's not that we have always done that particularly well; it's just that it wasn't part of the deal they thought they had signed up for.

Most of the UK church has been built around a deeply held commitment to the pastoral care contract. This is an unspoken and unwritten agreement that is based around the following simple points:

- It's the task of the leader to be clear about the future vision of the church.
- It's the task of the people to support, invest in and, at least in part, deliver this vision.
- In return, the people will be cared for.
- At times, people might test this level of care by absenting themselves from worship or being ill, not telling anyone and then complaining that the minister has not seen them.
- In some cases, this will be sealed with an agreement that only a visit from the church leader is an 'official' church visit. Anyone else does not count.

As long as there are vestiges of this pastoral care contract being practised, there will be inherent resistance to the concept of disciple-making.

In larger churches, it is normal for the task of pastoral care to be undertaken by specially trained and recognized members of a pastoral team, or leaders of small groups. But this does not remove the problem of the challenge to disciple-making; it simply transfers the contract to a different party.

The truth is that we need to help people see that when they join a local church, they are allowing themselves to be intentionally *discipled*. In line with God's desire that we grow into maturity, he calls us together into a community of fellow believers that is called the church in order to enable us to be formed as disciples of Jesus. This is the primary calling of church (Romans 12). It is true that we have a responsibility to care for one another – but the New Testament call is that this should be 'one to another'. Our primary need is not for professional, paid carers. We need strong networks of care that enable us to keep walking the path of discipleship.

This is the thrust of the teaching about ministry gifts in Ephesians 4:11–13. The gifts given to the church by the ascended Christ are people. These people carry, in themselves, the gifts and ministries of the Spirit that enable a community of people to engage in 'works of service' as well as grow into maturity. These ministries need to be varied: apostolic, prophetic, evangelistic, pastoral and didactic, precisely because the 'works of service' are varied and the maturing of disciples of Jesus is complex.

The fundamental role of church leaders is not to be the principal carers, nor the principal missionaries, nor the events managers for the local church. The fundamental role is to ensure that the community is a disciple-making one, a church that will help us to grow in maturity and mission. Therefore, this is a community that will not miss the opportunities that are offered to us by periods of ill health, unemployment, stress, discomfort, joy and excitement to ask the question: 'How might this be an arena where God could form me in Christ-likeness?'

The temptation is always to revert to type, to allow the church to concentrate on its own comfort, security and enjoyment. And the reason this is so much of a temptation is because it appeals to our selfish nature. Most of us are only ever a heartbeat away from the cry, 'What's in it for me?' The leader needs to be the one who constantly recalls the church to live out a more radical vocation: to be a congregation that knowingly and determinedly follows the way of Jesus.

I think that this is what Paul is doing in his epistles to Timothy. He left Timothy in Ephesus in a church that had become inward looking, concerned with genealogies and ascetic practices (1 Timothy 1:4; 4:3). This is a church that had forgotten its central purpose. It had become embroiled in internal concerns, forgetting that in the great city of Ephesus they were supposed to be living as salt and light. So after outlining his own testimony again (1:12–20), Paul directs the church to pray for those in authority (2:1–8). Once you begin to pray for the city leaders, you begin to take your eyes off yourselves and your own small quarrels.

And he has particular directions for Timothy. He is to point out to those who are the ascetics that 'everything God created is good' (4:4). He is not to get involved in their petty arguments (4:7; 6:20). Despite his age, he was to become an example of what a healthy, whole-life follower of Jesus was (4:12). He was to guard his relationships with people (5:1–2) and ensure that the most vulnerable were cared for. But his task was so much more than just 'caring' or providing religious services. Paul instructs Timothy to 'command and teach these things' (4:11). 'These things' include the call to live full lives with gratitude for all that God has created. Timothy's task was also to call people to lives of authentic godliness (4:7–8), made possible only through God's salvation (4:10). He was there to remind the church of its central purpose.

The opposite of the pastoral care contract is not that people do not care what is happening to us. Our situations are taken seriously but the questions we ask of one another are the deep questions that relate to our growth in Christ.

This needs careful work to explain to people. Only the very inexperienced or very naïve would think it helpful to announce to their congregation, 'I won't be involved in any pastoral care.' If people suspect their joys and challenges in life are unvalued, they will never grow as disciples. But if they see that the call to which we are all responding is that of being transformed in the midst of life into the likeness of Christ, they might grasp the possibilities of growth that they have in their own lives.

A different conversation

For this to be a reality, it will take leaders to understand how to formulate a mutually accepted disciple-making contract that will replace the traditional pastoral care contract.

I had been the guest speaker in a west London church the morning that Ed had led. After the service, he talked to me about his work situation. For two years he had worked in a context that he hated; he was overqualified for the job he was doing, felt demotivated and had asked God to get him out of the situation time and time again. Nothing had changed.

His great desire was to be able to serve God by becoming a full-time worship leader and he wanted to be trained at Hillsong, Australia. As far as he was concerned, his life was being wasted. He wasn't angry with God. He was just perplexed.

As we talked, I reminded him about the experience of the exiles and Jeremiah's advice to them when they felt they were in the wrong place, with the wrong people, when all they wanted to do was to escape. His direction to them was that they should settle down, and pray for the blessing of the people they found themselves among. And this was to happen, despite – and maybe because – the exiles felt they were in the wrong place (Jeremiah 29:7). Ed listened and we left each other.

When we met a few months later, he reminded me about our conversation. He had taken it to heart and decided to go to work fifteen minutes earlier than he had been doing. He spent the time with his workmates. They told their jokes, spoke about the football and local events. Nothing special. But over time, they began to find out that he was a Christian. Alongside the usual jokes, some people began to ask him to pray for their situations. Some began to ask about the part that faith played in his life. He had begun to see how God might use him. He still hated his job; he'd just found a bigger purpose in being there.

I didn't have any further contact with Ed after that conversation until I bumped into him at Spring Harvest a few years later. Things had changed for him. He had moved area, got a new job working with kids at risk of going off the rails and loved it. He reminded me of the conversations we had had in the past. He felt they had been crucial for him. The lessons he learned in those hard, frustrating days were still with him and had taught him to pray differently now that he was in the job he loved. He still led worship, but knew that he was also serving God where he was.

This is an encounter where it would have been easy to fall into a 'care' role – offering advice about switching jobs, praying again that God would change the situation, concentrating on the effect that this frustration was having on Ed.

But a disciple-making conversation sees that this is an opportunity too good to waste. We can leave people on the 'couch' but our calling is to get them out on the track, running the race. The very discomfort of the situation and the fact that God had not answered the prayer suggested that a better outcome was possible here. It wasn't about being uncaring about the situation; it was an opportunity to learn about life as a missionary disciple that would not be possible in other circumstances.

Of course, these conversations need wisdom. It needs courage on the part of the one asking the hard questions. It needs someone to be open to hear something that might not be what was hoped for. And it needs the right moment. You can't ask someone to identify the lessons they might be learning on the day they have been diagnosed with some dreadful disease. But at the right time, with the right tone, with the assurance of the best motives, the outcome can be a liberating one. It can lead to someone being equipped to make a difference where they are. It starts with the question that would always be asked. It's the intentionality and the direction of the subsequent conversation that demonstrates the desire to disciple people, as the following table shows.

Pastoring in a pastoral care model	Pastoring in a pastoral equipping model
How are you feeling?	How are you feeling?
Why is this happening?	How can you respond to what is happening?
Where is God?	What is God doing?
When will this end?	What do you need so that you don't miss this opportunity to grow?
Who can support you so you get through this?	Who can support you in this situation so that you can be most fruitful in it?
Can we get you back to 'normality' so that you can 'move on'?	Can we help you integrate what has happened to you into your ongoing life as a disciple?

2. A change in the psychology of the relationship between leaders and people

The concept of every Christian being a 'minister', able to be equipped to do the work of ministry, wherever they find themselves, is almost universally accepted. The Reformation's belief in the 'priesthood of all believers' is acknowledged almost as a truism. However, the underlying assumptions of the roles that are played may suggest a different set of priorities.

The following was a point made by Mark Gibbs in 1981:

> Even where the theology of a common calling is accepted, the *psychology* of a partnership between clergy and laity is still difficult, even in the most Protestant churches. I have had the privilege of visiting a considerable number of seminaries in the last few years; and I must report that even where the priesthood of all believers is central to their beliefs, I have found sometimes an assumption among young clergy and seminarians that the laity are still objects to be done good to, and that we are children that must be taught new tricks, that we are immature people not to be trusted with really controversial and difficult doctrines. I have detected also that some clergy are comfortable when they are dealing with weak and dependent and needy laity, but that they are not very happy with strong, mature and well-informed laity.[1]

Is that fair? Perhaps we would all like to think that this may happen in some places, but not where we are.

The truth is that church leaders spend most of their time dealing with two groups of people: people in pain and people with leadership responsibilities in the church.

These conversations cannot be dismissed lightly. The people in pain are those who have hit crises in their lives with which they need help. These range over the whole of the spectrum of life's journey: the challenges of adolescence, the sweet-sour pain of relationships, the life stages of marriage and birth, the disappointments of work, the betrayals in relationships, the uncertainty of illness, the paralysing power of grief. Just to begin to list the issues can provide an overwhelming sense of challenges to which the leaders are called to respond. These are major events and in even average-sized congregations, they can take the bulk of a leader's time. The danger for the leader is that he (or she) is looked to for advice, wisdom and guidance. The hope is that the leader will know what to do in all these situations. And he may feel he does know. But subtly, over time, it becomes easy to believe that leaders know what to do, while church members don't.

The other people who receive much time are those who have responsibilities in church. They might be those who share the responsibility for leadership, or those who will be the next generation of leaders. And it is vital that these conversations continue; without them the church will begin to weaken. In voluntary organizations such as the church, the currency of rewards is different than in business. Here the reward for service is often perceived to be access to the church leader – they get more of their time or perhaps more investment in their spiritual development than others or they are party to 'inside' information – they know what is *really* happening in the church. Leaders need the active support and involvement of the volunteers; the volunteers are rewarded by a sense of significance and satisfaction that the church is operating fruitfully.

The effect of these emphases has had a profound effect on the ministry of most church leaders. It's not difficult to understand how sermons are shaped, even if subconsciously, by the conversations that have taken most of the preacher's time during a week. It is therefore no surprise that the application of most teaching or preaching has been either pastorally focused or directed to the internal life of the church.

Nor is it surprising that in many people's eyes the minister is the person with the expertise that is most highly prized in church contexts: pastoral response and church direction.

But what about the rest of the people, indeed the majority of the church? The people who are just getting on with their lives? Those who do not ask to be seen? Those who seem to 'have it all together'? When does the pastor get time to hear what is happening to them? When does the pastor hear what God is doing through them or how they are being shaped by the events in their lives?

What would be learned from these 'experts' out on their frontlines if pastors took the time to listen to their situations? There are a myriad contexts that people are dealing with every day where their discipleship is being tested and stretched and lived out with authenticity. Leaders are missing out on the conversations about these places because they are too busy, and because their people don't think they are interested. So, initiating conversations about life 'out there' would be a sign to a church that everything matters to God, and by extension, to the people of God. Our growth as disciples will be enabled, and our churches will become disciple-making churches.

St Mary's is a large church in a rural setting, though with a high percentage of people in the community commuting to the nearby cities. Over the years the church has grown through offering services with which families have found it easy to connect. One of the challenges we identified at the beginning of the Imagine Project was that there were concerns about how these families could be encouraged to see themselves as whole-life disciples. The vicar spent a lot of time listening to the congregation as they explained about the pressures they faced, wanting to understand the pressures, but also wanting people to understand that it was among these very pressures where God could use them and shape them.

Three years later the vicar is still making himself available to people. Recently he hired the function room in one of the local pubs to have a 'Tell the vicar' session. He invited people to come and explain about their employment situations, as well as their challenges at home and in the neighbourhood. And people came. And he learned. And the congregation saw a minister wanting to learn. In the midst of a very busy diary full of civic duties, pastoral needs and church demands, he has demonstrated that if he is to take seriously the call to equip people as disciples, he has to listen to them and be seen to take their situations seriously.

The stark truth is that if as leaders we are determined to engage in a wider range of conversations, and our diaries are full, we will need to make some strategic choices in order to free space to pay attention to people. But if we have accepted the fact that we are a community of missionaries, then it becomes natural for us to want to know what is happening through one another.

The challenge is expressed well here:

Laity are those members of the church whom God has called to the church outside the walls of the church. In unison they might say, 'We write the laws of our land and invent new technologies to serve humanity. We know how to clone animals and humans and measure germs on Mars. We rear and educate children. We work in corporations, governments, and health care systems. We build roads and homes. We write and produce movies and TV shows. In those endeavors, we seek to practice our faith. We need the wisdom of faith through deeper theological reflection to help discern the how and why of it all.'[2]

The relationship between those in recognized church leadership and those in church membership will need to be recognized as a partnership of mission. It is clearly true that there will always be opportunities for corporate mission and they need to be taken. Leaders need to be able to identify these openings and ensure that the gathered church's response is a thoughtful and effective one. But there also needs to be a humble acknowledgment that there are many places where the people of God can go to be a blessing that would be closed to the paid leaders of the church.

For their part, leaders need the confidence in the work of the Spirit who will enable people to be used by him in his work. And the people, for their part, need the confidence to believe that God has placed them in contexts where his will and purpose can be furthered. For this to be a reality, there need to be relationships that reflect the hopes and the expertise of everyone. This relationship will be characterized by mutual, attentive listening.

3. A change in the leaders' focus

Most church leaders know their locality really well. They may be invited to become governors of local schools. They may get to know their neighbourhood police or health teams. They can become important community leaders. They can find themselves coopted onto local government bodies. The best of these leaders get under the skin of their com munity. They walk the streets, they know the rhythms of the neighbourhood, they are known by people outside the church. At their best, they are the welcoming 'face' of their local congregation.

And they see more opportunities for missional engagement than they have resources for. There may be more schools wanting Christian input than there are Christians available during the day. There may be more possibilities of ministering to the elderly and the vulnerable than there are hours in the day. So what the leader looks for is the availability of more people to be involved in the locality.

In a diagram, it might look like this:

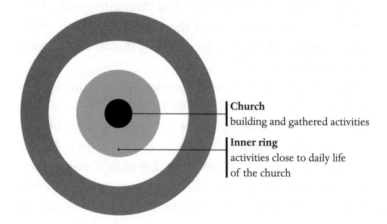

Church
building and gathered activities

Inner ring
activities close to daily life
of the church

If the bullseye is the church building or worship space and reflects most of the activities of the gathered church, the inner ring represents the activities of the church that are closely linked to its geographical location. So this might refer to lunch clubs for the elderly, visitation programmes, after-schools work, children's ministries and so on.

But alongside this work, there is a danger of becoming too parochial. So the church may be aware of its calling in the global scene. There are serious issues that we get concerned about: issues of justice, poverty, disaster and politics. These issues never stop. The media does a good job of presenting what is happening overseas with a relentlessness that can leave us feeling powerless. But we can pray and we can give finance and we can raise awareness. And these are important.

A diagram would portray these twin concerns in this way:

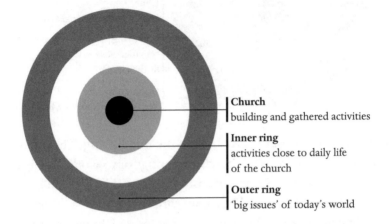

Church
building and gathered activities

Inner ring
activities close to daily life of the church

Outer ring
'big issues' of today's world

The outer ring reflects the concerns we have for national and international issues – famine, disasters, AIDS. This, along with the central ring, receives most of the attention in church life. We recruit people for the activities in and around the church, and these activities receive money from our budgets. The international situations get our attention in prayer and special giving. Both are really important responses for a church.

However, the reality is that many people can end up feeling distanced from international events, praying with little faith that they can really make a difference. At the same time, they may not be able to get involved in activities that are geographically close to the church, because they are not around at the time when their services might be needed, or they may just live at a distance from the church and only go to the locality when they meet to worship. So they end up feeling as though they are uninvolved in its ministry.

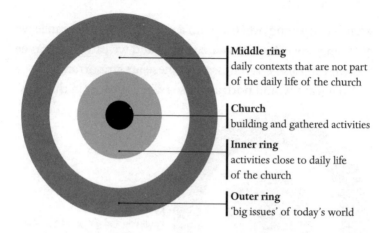

Middle ring
daily contexts that are not part
of the daily life of the church

Church
building and gathered activities

Inner ring
activities close to daily life
of the church

Outer ring
'big issues' of today's world

They spend most of their time in the middle ring. They may commute distances to church gatherings or to work, and feel that church life is separated from the place they live and have their leisure time in. They may simply not have a sense of calling to the area where the church is located. In the past they may have felt a little guilty whenever someone asked, 'If the church weren't here, would anyone miss us?'

It's a reasonable question, but only if it's understood properly. Of course what we do together matters, and we have a responsibility to extend kindness, love and grace to the neighbourhood community around the church. But if this is all that is being asked, the question is too small. However, if we ask whether anyone would miss the difference offered by the scattered members of the church in the communities they spend time in (work, school, clubs) if they weren't there, then the question is a good one. We need to be challenged to make a difference in both our gathered and our scattered forms.

Leaders need to be able to be realistic about how to keep all three rings (inner, middle and outer) in appropriate tension. And that tension will differ according to the local congregation. Churches with a lot of local people with time available may well be glad to get involved in local matters. Other churches might have to realize that their ministry is more likely to be in the middle ring. They may be a congregation where most work full-time, commute to work and are time-poor.

Leaders need to feel the freedom not to have to do everything. We do not need to be a local church that responds to every need. We have to be at ease about how we enable people to live missionally – not driven by the need, but called by the opportunity that life presents.

Wise leaders will recognize that while they may be almost totally engaged in the direct locality of the church, they need to allow their ministry to be part of the overall ministry of the church. They have to curb the temptation to make their work sound as though it's the most important work. They have to see themselves as part of the body of Christ, with their work as part of the overall work of the church. A vital part, but only a part.

Before you switch off . . .

For some leaders, this is the moment you might want to laugh and remind me what life is like 'in the real world'. There are only so many hours in the week; there are so many demands on your time; your life may be dominated by duties that you would never choose to be engaged with out of personal preference, so where do you get the time?

I think it is important to be realistic here and also acknowledge that it is not necessarily about doing more. So, for example, if you need to spend time with the treasurer about the church finances, it's not difficult to find space in that conversation to ask what she thinks God might be doing in her workplace. These sorts of insight are worth listening to.

This has to be done in one-to-one conversations, but imagine what could happen if the principle was also modelled in gathered church settings.

The dreaded AGM or church meeting, or something equally exciting

Depending on your tradition, you might have regular church business meetings, or annual meetings, or vision-casting events. Whatever they are called, they often have certain things in common. They are times when church activities are reported and prayed for, and support is encouraged. Anyone listening could easily imagine that this is all that 'the church' is doing. What would such a meeting look like if we were to take seriously the opportunities and challenges faced by members of the congregation in their everyday lives? The pragmatist's immediate response is to ask how long the meeting would be. Well, it could be long, or you could choose where the emphasis of the evening was. What it would mean is that everyone would be clear that the church in both its gathered and its scattered forms has rich missional possibilities.

What would leadership meetings look like if, instead of just reporting on pastoral situations, each meeting had as part of the agenda reports back on how disciples were being made? A simple change in the agenda would reflect a significant culture shift. Indeed, in one Anglican church we worked with, a decision was made, as mentioned earlier, that the question 'What progress are we making in making whole-life disciples?' should be posed to the paid team at every church business meeting. More broadly, we observed the following:

> In all the churches we worked with, the primary question that was asked at each consultation meeting was 'How are we

doing?' Not simply in terms of attendance, or building concerns or relational issues, but in terms of the intentional development of disciples. One interesting observation concerning this was that often church leadership groups did not have an agreed way of measuring this. So the answer began to centre on stories that had been shared of people making a difference and being changed because of the situations they were facing. The very act of asking the question provoked a new way of thinking.

The central change in this psychology between the leader and the people is that the leader is able to acknowledge that he or she is not the expert on all things faith-based. Leaders can sit easily with the gifts that they have, but are eager to acknowledge that they are part of the body of Christ, not the head of it. As such they have gifts to offer people needing to live out the gospel in the world: theological insight, perspective that comes from knowing some church history, spiritual discernment that comes from being trained in Christian disciplines and so on. However, they need to have the security that allows them to learn from the congregation how this all works out in the everyday arena. We need to be partners in mission.

Develop a new awareness of the challenges that people face

In many cases, leaders are aware of what is being faced by many of the congregation, but it may be less common for people to be aware of each other's situations. It is remarkably common to find communities that have never taken the time to ask one another significant questions.

I spent one evening with a congregation going through the issues that people had named as being particularly challenging for them. A range of issues had been named, though none was particularly remarkable or unexpected – things like struggles with debt, aging parents, health. As I was going through the list, I asked whether people knew to whom these problems referred.

One might expect people in larger congregations to be less aware of challenges being faced by individuals. But that evening, it quickly became clear that even in this small church, people had no appreciation of the issues. They expected their pastor to know, but they had never created the space to have these conversations.

One man said to me at the end of the evening, 'What I've realized tonight is that we like each other, but we don't really know each other.'

Their response was to spend the next six weeks in their small groups allowing each other to tell their stories and to be prayed for. They already had an infrastructure that would allow for these conversations; it's just that they had never had the motivation to do so before.

One direct result of these conversations saw one of the retired men in the church coming to realize that his frontline was his weekly visit to an older friend living in sheltered housing. The group began to pray for him, he realized the potential significance of the visits and he approached these visits with a sense of how God might be able to use him.

That is why doing the survey is so significant. A whole church can receive a wake-up call when it knows about the lives of those who belong to it. And leaders can hear about the issues that people are really having to deal with. Indeed, listening becomes one of the most significant signs that we are taking seriously the call to love one another.

But the type of listening we long to see is 'listening to learn', not listening as a precursor to offering solutions. This can be refreshing, because it is a chance to hear the realities of the everyday experiences of others. There need be no rush to make a considered response. Indeed, the church leader needs to understand that he or she is not the expert in this conversation proffering nuggets of wisdom, but rather the interested, inquisitive party armed with good questions, ready to be surprised at what is discovered. Without this kind of spirit, we will never be able to reflect truly what it means to be a community, nor will we be able to begin to understand the pressures and opportunities that we face when we are scattered. However, with this intention, there can be a freedom to learn, and we are relieved of the pressure of having to respond with solutions.

How can this happen?

Let me suggest some ideas that we have seen in action:

- Some leaders have begun to travel in to work with church members, learning to appreciate again the wearying aspects of a daily commute. For many of the churches we worked with, their biggest frustration was the length of commuting time that many of the church community had. This means that working days are lengthened, leisure time is limited and people are more tired. Sustaining a sense of God's presence in busy commuter trains is an art, and one that many church leaders have forgotten. To experience it again was salutary for those willing to do it.
- Others have visited people at work. One church has three members of staff, not all of them full-time. However, as part of their role, each of them has to meet a different member of the congregation each Wednesday at lunchtime. But this has to happen on the church

member's territory: in or around their workplace, in their home or in the cafés they prefer to meet in. This means that every week, paid church staff are hearing stories of people's frontlines. It's a chance for them to learn.

- Others have gone one stage further and have been able to 'shadow' people at work, seeing what they face day by day. Everyone who has done this testifies that it changed their understanding of their congregation, and altered their understanding of their ministry as church leaders.

- Many churches have long had pastoral teams who respond to people facing difficulties in their own lives. Perhaps inevitably, the emphasis of these teams has been on care. But some have begun to see that they could be used more proactively. Rather than waiting for difficulties, teams could be encouraged to meet people to find out what is happening in their 110 hours and more specifically on their missional frontline. Rather than just responding to pastoral crises, they could enable new conversations and celebrate when things are going well. Pastoral care could be given a much wider meaning than many have imagined up to the present time.

Small groups, intentional conversations over coffee after the service and planned visits can all be used to listen to people's stories. The method is not as important as the fact that the body of Christ gets a chance to hear the stories of life on the frontline. We need to be partners in learning.

Facing some truths

Though there is a central need to address the relationship between church leaders and congregations, there are some truths that need to be faced and costs to be paid, as the following shows.

The truth	The cost
Some church leaders enjoy being the missional hero, whose role is to recruit volunteers to their vision.	The fact that some people may feel that their 110-hour zone is the primary missional arena may mean that there will never be enough personnel resources to respond to all the opportunities of which the church leader is aware.
Some people are happy to let the church leader be the missional hero, whose role is either to do everything or to come up with the ideas for future ventures.	Some people might resist the change in emphasis or be initially confused by what is expected of them.
Some leaders are introverts and find these conversations hard work.	Some good work is hard work!
Most leaders are already busy; they can't see where the time will come from.	Some priorities may need to change; a new perspective will also mean that existing conversations may have different outcomes.

The central question concerns whether the prize of seeing the development of a whole-life disciple-making community is worth the cost involved. If a church is to become a whole-life disciple-making church, its members will see their leader redefine and change his or her role. It will be a role that is formed by a sober assessment of the leader's gifts, a necessary humility that is exhibited in the art of asking questions so that he or she will understand more, and a desire for the relationship between leader and people to be mutually strengthening. The temptations to be the hero, to do things for or to people, will be put to one side, and replaced by a determination to see leadership as one necessary gift given to the body, to be used alongside all the other gifts.

If I had been able to grasp what this might have looked like in a local church all those years ago, it would not have made my task as a leader any easier, but it might not have resulted in the burnout I experienced. I might have been a different leader.

> We made some small changes that concretely expressed our commitment to whole-life discipleship, and that opened up bigger things for us. For example, up to that time, if anyone went on the mission field or to Bible college we would have them up on stage to pray for them to commission them because it was 'God's call', and it is God's call. But seeing things in a new light, we changed. Now if anyone gets a new job or has promotion or goes to university, we pray because that is 'God's call' too. So, if someone gets a job in Asda we get them up on stage to commission them and pray for them that they would be the best Asda worker that Asda has ever had in Dewsbury!
> Leader, Imagine Pilot Church

Pause for thought

If you're a leader:

1. How do you react to this chapter? Does it resonate with the expectations that you feel others have of you?
2. What can you do to begin to change the existing situation?
3. With whom do you need to begin this conversation?

If you're not a leader:

4. How do you react to this chapter? Does it resonate with your expectations of a church leader?

5. Why do you think this situation has developed?
6. How can it begin to change in your church?
7. With whom do you need to talk?

Further reading

Peterson, Eugene, *Practice Resurrection* (Eerdmans, 2010).
Roxburgh, Alan and Romanuk, Fred, *The Missional Leader* (Jossey-Bass, 2006).
Walton, Roger, *The Reflective Disciple* (Epworth, 2009).
Simple Church: www.simplechurch.eu

*We need to build and strengthen mature communities
of vision and character who celebrate faith as a way of life
as they **gather** before God for worship and who,
sent by God, live it out as they **scatter** to pursue
various tasks in the world.*

M. Volf, 'The Church's Great Malfunctions',
Christianity Today, October 2006

6

How the whole-life DNA changes things: three examples

For those of us who are part of the traditional format of church, despite our historical differences, we have much in common. The move to becoming a whole-life church is not only a possibility for a certain type of church. It can happen regardless of social setting, denominational tradition, size of congregation or age profile. The only prerequisite for change to happen is a fundamental shift in our perspective. This will demand a culture change which will mean that our actions have to change. But it starts with how you approach your everyday situations with a new lens: the whole-life lens.

To demonstrate that, I want to explore three areas of church life that we all have in common. The first is what could happen on a Sunday morning. The second suggests a different way of looking at our mundane tasks in church and the final one demonstrates how people begin to view their everyday lives differently.

1. Whole-life Sunday mornings

Sunday worship gets a bad press in many Christian circles. There may be much about the format of Sunday mornings that is problematic, but for many 'ordinary' churches, it is still the moment in the week when most of the church community gather to worship together. So this seems like a good place to start thinking about the difference a number of one-degree shifts would make.

We have emphasized continually that the key thing to introduce is not another bolt-on programme, but a whole new perspective on our life together. You may do the things that you have always done, but the difference is that everything will be reflecting the wider perspective of whole-life. Maybe one way to help make this concrete is to provide two different approaches to the Sunday morning worship experience of 'AnyTown Church' – a typical Sunday morning event, and then a different perspective on what might happen if their culture was different.

These two portraits are not designed to be caricatures but they are presented to describe two different approaches. As we have seen, the culture of any church or group is formed by the language we use, the expectations we bring, the actions we take and the assumptions we build on. The first portrait, the one we might think of as more usual, is not neutral. In fact, it militates against whole-life discipleship. The second presentation doesn't simply tweak a few of the elements in the service, but rather expresses some fundamental differences in theology and therefore in culture. What is worth pointing out is that we have not added anything to the second service; we have just seen everything through a different lens.

Our church traditions have their own liturgical elements and they are valued for good reason. Whatever yours may be, the challenge is to consider prayerfully how your tradition, whether sacramental, reformed or charismatic, enables people to leave the service with a bigger vision of God, the Lordship of Jesus and the part that they have to play as faithful whole-life disciples.

It should be clear that the two services will leave people with different impressions of what it means to live for God. There may be much that is similar; at their best people will be pleased that they have been together with others, though the second will have offered the chance for people to become aware of the circumstances that others are facing.

The worship in each might be equally uplifting, but in the first it may have been understood to be a welcome escape from the everyday pressures that are being faced. The engagement with the Bible will have left people aware of Joseph's life and challenges, though only the second will have seen that story grounded in the day-to-day life of people in the congregation facing similar pressures. In addition, it's possible that the first sermon, emphasizing the 'rescue' motif, could easily become unhitched from the gospel narrative that we see played out in the life of Jesus; whereas the second sermon, in seeking to take seriously the reality of the situations facing people, actually mirrors the experience of Jesus who denounced power, seemed to have lost everything, but was vindicated by God.

It is hard to overemphasize how significant it is that our experience of gathered worship reflects the desire to be a whole-life disciple-making community. Ultimately, this is all about the flow of life that comes from the work of God in us through salvation, the life that flows through us by the power of the Spirit in and for the sake of the world, which he loves so much.

Though it can be misunderstood as simply making a few verbal adjustments, it's actually about cultivating a conscious self-awareness that means that our life together can become

Sunday morning at AnyTown Church where there is no relationship between 10 and 110.

Greeting: You're met at the door and welcomed warmly, pass the noticeboard with the posters advertising various church events in the area, along with the missionary noticeboard highlighting people and agencies working abroad. The heading on the board is: 'Therefore go and make disciples of all nations . . .'

News sheet: You collect a news sheet with lists of the events that will be happening in and around the church building. Your eyes glaze over as there is yet another request 'for hands that do dishes . . .' and you hum the tune to yourself. And you smile because you didn't think you could remember it.

Chatter: You meet your friends and catch up on the week, listening while they tell you about the challenges of teenagers, sick cats, difficult bosses and aching backs.

Worship: Then someone interrupts by calling you to your seats, encouraging you with the words, 'Let's leave everything that we've been involved with this week behind. Let's just concentrate on Jesus.' Your back aches as you stand to sing, 'Let everything that has breath praise the Lord.'

Prayer: Someone prays that God will come and meet you, that you will hear from God, that you will understand who God is.

Worship: You sing for a while longer. The PowerPoint slides have nice sunset or waterfall scenes on them, though they don't make up for the spelling mistakes.

Notices: Someone comes and spends time telling you what is going to be happening in the church this week, encouraging you to attend prayer meetings for the upcoming mission event, and to attend the home groups that are nearest to your home. You're reminded of the people who are sick and away from church.

Children: The children leave to go to their own activities. They'll listen to a biblical story, get involved in some creative activities, hear a prayer, and sing a song. They're glad to be leaving.

Sermon: The preacher is in the middle of a series on Joseph. We're up to Genesis 47:13–31. The sermon is all about dealing with crises in our lives. You're encouraged to:

- discover God's purposes (he wants to rescue people);
- discover God's plans (he had a plan for the Israelites and he used Joseph's gifts); and
- discover God's power (God was greater than the famine).

Song: To help you respond to the sermon, you close by singing, 'What a faithful God have I.'

Coffee: You all shuffle through to the hall to get some coffee, which you serve yourselves from flasks. You grab some biscuits and find someone to chat to, and end up talking about the football.

Sunday morning at AnyTown Church where there is a real attempt to form a relationship between 10 and 110.

Greeting: You're met at the door and welcomed warmly, pass the noticeboard with the posters advertising various church events in the area, along with a large map indicating where the congregation spend most of their time in the week. This sits alongside pictures of the overseas missionaries. The heading on the board is: 'Therefore go and make disciples of all nations . . .'

News sheet: You collect a news sheet with lists of the events happening this week. Along with requests for help with the dishes, you're encouraged to pray for someone who's got a new job. You find yourself humming the tune, 'Hi ho, hi ho, it's off to work I go . . .' and you smile because you didn't think you could remember it.

Chatter: You meet your friends and catch up on the week, listening while they tell you about the challenges of teenagers, sick cats, difficult bosses and aching backs.

Worship: Then someone interrupts by calling you to your seats, encouraging you to 'recognize Jesus is the Lord of all that we've been involved with this week'. Your back aches as you stand to sing, 'Let everything that has breath praise the Lord.'

Prayer: Someone offers thanks that God has been with you all week in every situation, and has been working in you and through you. They pray that today you will hear from God, understanding who he is, so you can live more fully for him.

Worship: You sing for a while longer. The PowerPoint slides include pictures of your town, though they don't make up for the spelling mistakes.

Notices: Someone comes and encourages everyone to attend prayer meetings for the ongoing mission of the church, which also includes an upcoming church mission event. As well as being reminded about home groups, you're asked to pray for the people who are sick and away from church. You pray for Elsie, just retired from working as a school secretary, that God will find her a new frontline and that she'll be fruitful there.

Children: The children leave to go to their own activities. They'll listen to one another's news, hear how the week has been, listen to a biblical story, get involved in some creative activities, think about how the story will help them live differently this week, hear a prayer and sing a song. They're glad to be leaving.

Sermon: The preacher is in the middle of a series on Joseph. We're up to Genesis 47:13–31. We are encouraged to:

- remember God's purpose;
- resist being conformed to the culture; and
- reject ruthlessness when we are in positions of power.

One woman speaks about her life as a boss and the challenges she faces.

Song: To help you respond to the sermon, you close by singing, 'Come, now is the time to worship.'

Coffee: You all shuffle through to the hall to get some coffee, which is served by a team of people who make sure that, armed with biscuits, you have someone to talk to. You find yourselves talking about times you've been tempted to blend into the background at work, unlike Joseph. You chat on and end up talking about the football.

dramatically releasing for everyone, as they engage in their whole lives as followers of Jesus.

2. Whole-life coffee rotas

Once you see the formation of whole-life missionary disciples as being the church community's primary task, then everything can be seen through that filter.

Take something mundane, like being part of the church coffee rota. What might serving on the coffee rota have to do with mission on the frontline? Well, the encouraging thing about the decision to make whole-life disciples is that a whole host of things that we already do in church can become the means to train people to be more fruitful out in their frontlines.

This is a suggested take on how the coffee rota task might become a tool for mission inside and outside the church, inspired by Mark Greene.

What's the job description for the coffee rota? Probably something like this:

10.00:	Lay out ninety mugs, eight plates for biscuits, thirty-five beakers. Load coffee machine with coffee.
10.20:	Turn on water boiler.
10.28:	Check water is heating, go to service.
11.30:	Leave worship service. Put biscuits on plates, make squash for kids, get out milk, sugar and so on. Put on coffee machine.
11.42:	Brew tea.
11.45:	Service ends, service begins.
12.15:	Start clearing up: begin washing up, put cups away.

That's the job description but surely that's not the job. Yes, all those tasks have to be done; however, serving coffee isn't really about getting caffeine into people's veins, but about getting people into good conversations. We don't urge people to stay for coffee at the end of a service because we fear that they'll collapse from dehydration after sitting through a service. The coffee time is not about coffee at all – you can tell that by the standard of the coffee that is sometimes served.

The coffee time is about creating a space where relationships can be formed and strengthened. And beyond that the job of the people on the rota ought to be about spotting who needs an encouraging word, who needs someone to talk to, who might need prayer. The job is to look down the queue and be thinking, 'Jim doesn't look too happy today. I wonder if there's something wrong. I'll spend a couple of extra seconds with him but when he's past, I'll signal to John and suggest he goes over and makes sure Jim's all right.'

Of course, that has to be done discreetly. There are few things more effective in making someone feel low than telling them that they look low, ill, tired, depressed, wrung out or strung out.

But later John gives you a smile and a thumbs-up sign.

The coffee rota team is on the frontline of pastoral reconnaissance and care.

And then there are the visitors. As the coffee rota person sees a newcomer in the queue, they've got a couple of glances and then maybe forty seconds as they serve them to work out who in the congregation might be best to connect them with. 'Well,' they're thinking, 'she looks as if she's in her mid-thirties, no ring on her second finger, well-cut hair, tanned face but much whiter hands – probably professional, single and recently been skiing . . . Well, Jean loves skiing . . . ' And afterwards they find out they were wrong . . . about the skiing, at least. The visitor hadn't been skiing but did own a soft-top

Spitfire Mark 1V and drove with gloves . . . and it had been a gloriously sunny weekend.

So the coffee rota team are not only the frontline of relationship-building and pastoral reconnaissance; they are also on the frontline of visitor hospitality. And although you may not have Sherlock Holmes or Miss Marple tendencies, as one church leader put it, 'If people knew the job was about actually making a difference, quite a lot more people might want to do it.'

But still, what's that got to do with training people for mission on the frontline?

Well, fast forward from Sunday morning to Monday morning, 8.20 am. A mum is trundling up to the school gate with her ten-year-old daughter. At the school gate she can see sixty other mums . . . she knows around forty of them. 'Which one,' she wonders, as she surveys their body language and their facial expressions, 'which one might need a word? Which one might God be directing me to talk to right now?'

Or it's 8.20 and you arrive at your office and there are thirty people there. You can shout 'hello' to everyone, but who needs a word, who do you need to look out for today, who does someone else need to look out for today?

And you think, 'If only I'd been trained on the coffee rota, then I'd have had a lot of practice at this. But there was a two-year waiting list for a slot . . . '

What we do in church often has much potential to help us develop transferable skills, transferable perspectives and transferable attitudes for our mission on the frontline. The opportunity is not only to know that but to identify pro-actively how everything we do might serve that external missional purpose more effectively.

Of course, there is a danger that all this could appear quite patronizing – but we underestimate the value of being members of a learning community. The attitudes and behaviours we learn and practise in church can be offered out in the 110 and enable people who are not Christians to see new ways of living – the teacher who says 'sorry' to a pupil for a mistake, the accountant who notices a supplier's mistake in their favour and tells them, the carpenter who always does his hours unlike the rest of the team and so on.

When we're living as whole-life disciples out in the world, these actions need to come before explanations for our actions. And it's these actions that disciples can learn in the context of their local church. For those who are aware of these possibilities, every role taken in the local church can be linked to the skills needed for whole-life missionary discipleship. For this to happen, it needs someone to explain what is happening. Someone needs to invest the mundane with a bigger purpose.

3. Whole-life living

The goal of all this is the releasing of the people of God to embrace all that God can do in and through them on their frontlines. This is the goal of all this work – that people might feel commissioned to love people, serve with their whole strength and discern what God is doing there.

The goal looks like ordinary people living with a sense of their role in what God wants to do in and around them.

There's a bus driver who's passionate about serving people. Albert has a natural way of extending courtesies that make life easier – waiting for the person who's still running to the stop, exercising patience with those who've lost their change.

He's also bothered about the other drivers in the depot. Not long ago, he returned to work after a short strike during which only five drivers had crossed the picket line. He knew what he had to do. 'My job tomorrow,' he said, 'is to be a peacemaker. That's why I'm here.'

Albert had a vision to make a difference in his place of work. Quietly spoken, with a sense of humour, a diplomat and a good listener, he used his gifts by actively engaging with the relational tensions of his workplace. Along the way he hopes to drive lots of people safely from A to B, to enable as many as possible to experience grace through his attention to their needs and to speak about Jesus as the one who inspires his vision for a life worth living.

What gave Albert the vision for this approach to life? It may have happened with direct encouragement from his church, or in spite of it. But with the goal of moving towards becoming a whole-life church, the hope is that there will be more people like Albert who feel equipped to live their everyday lives in the light of their mission. The more that people can begin to reclaim a vision for their own front-lines, the more they are likely to be aware of what God is doing.

It starts as an individual sees his or her fundamental identity as being a disciple of Jesus. When this is settled, people can begin to see the creative ways that they can serve God in their situations, for his glory.

The above are three small examples that each take the everyday realities but want to see them through a new per-spective: the whole-life disciple-making perspective.

Discipleship took a new twist after an Imagine Saturday morning workshop. Andy and Johnny and I agreed to start meeting as a discipleship triplet – a grand title for three mates grabbing a coffee together. We meet at the local McDonald's. It's great just to take a bit of time out to meet with supportive friends.

We're dads, we are busy with work, and we share a desire to be better followers of Jesus. We talk about the challenges of family life, work, relationships, decision-making, etc. It's good to catch up and share experiences about the pressures and opportunities we face. In essence, I suppose we are trying to apply our Christian faith to the nitty-gritty of life.

The best question we ask each other is, 'What should we pray for you?' This never fails to flush out the key issues in our lives. We keep on praying and texting each other with special requests. Church member, Imagine Pilot Church

Pause for thought

1. Think about the last worship service you attended. How could it have been led in a way that reflected a whole-life perspective?
2. Think about the tasks you are involved with in church life. What discipleship skills are you gaining that will enable you to live as a whole-life disciple when you are away from church?

Further reading

Cotterell, Tracy and Greene, Mark, *Let My People Grow* (Authentic, 2006).

Wilhoit, Jim, *Spiritual Formation as if the Church Mattered* (Baker, 2008).

Witherington, Ben, *Work: A Kingdom Perspective on Labour* (Eerdmans, 2011).

Imagine Project: www.licc.org.uk/imagine

The word 'now' is like a bomb through the window,
and it ticks.

Arthur Miller

7

As you begin . . .

By this stage, the hope is that you've had a chance to reflect on the stories that have been presented, recognized the process of handling change and been encouraged as you realize that you're already part-way down this road of becoming a whole-life church. The encouragement that we have is that we know change can happen, with ordinary people in ordinary churches facing ordinary challenges.

And there is a whole range of challenges, but these need not be overwhelming. There may be a long period before people accept the responsibility that this vision offers them, but the clock can start from this moment. There are steps that can be taken right now.

Are you ready to face the challenges?

There are at least five challenges facing any church wanting to become an environment where whole-life disciples are nurtured, equipped, sustained and celebrated. These need to be acknowledged. However, they do not need to present insuperable barriers.

The challenge of people recognizing that this is what being a Christian means

As has been said, discipleship is an easily misunderstood word. For too many people, it remains an intimidating concept. It sounds as though it is reserved for the keenest of Christians, those likely to go on retreats, read books with lofty thoughts, spend hours in prayer. Somewhere along the way we have divorced the concepts of what it means to be a Christian and what it means to be a disciple, and have forgotten that what it means to be a disciple is to follow Jesus in all of life.

Therefore, it is no surprise that many have little imagination to embrace the possibility that God would be able to use them in their everyday life for his purposes, or that God would engage in shaping their lives through mundane activities.

The challenge of the inward pull of gathered church

Nothing that we have written about here is new – but it has rarely been embraced by whole congregations. Historically, communities have found it very difficult to resist the inward pull focusing on the gathered church. This pull encourages people to be more concerned about the functioning of the community than its purpose. People easily begin to feel that the important spiritual activities take place in the midst of the gathered congregation, and that to be caught up in activities away from this community is to be dominated by 'secular' concerns which are, by definition, things that are outside the orbit of God's dynamic interest.

This radically reduces the likelihood that Christians will seek intentionally, persistently and prayerfully to make a difference out in the world.

The challenge to the role of leaders

A primary component of the role of leaders is to help equip the people of God for their ministry. In many cases this will mean that leaders will need to develop new skills in listening, spiritual direction and motivation. Alongside this, the criteria of successful ministry will change. No longer will it be about what they are doing themselves. Success will be marked by the number of people who have embraced their own frontlines as their arenas for ministry and are living fruitfully there. If all this is to be the case, the activities of the leaders must change to meet these new challenges – not least in their own learning.

Leaders who are very capable in theological and biblical matters may feel ill-equipped to help people reflect theologically on their everyday lives. Some leaders may struggle with a sense that it would be better to carry on working harder in the ways they have always worked, rather than opening themselves up to a new set of questions and opportunities to learn. Pastors and people must learn to learn new things and learn to learn from one another.

The challenge of sustaining change

We have found that many congregations are quick to understand the need to create a community that is fruitful in both gathered and scattered modes. They themselves have been able to come up with the changes that will address the central issues. However, it's one thing to begin to address an issue; it's another to keep going until whole-life thinking becomes a natural and self-sustaining response. That takes longer and it's easy to underestimate how long that process really takes.

If a church has had no expectation that its life should be about anything other than a pastoral unit, with occasional forays into corporate mission activity, the first year of this process will be taken up in simply outlining the vision, encouraging people to see the implications of it for their own lives and implementing the most obvious of one-degree shifts.

The second and third years will be a process of embedding this new culture in the life of the church. Our experience is that during this time, the new practices may still feel unnatural and at times artificial. It will probably be around the fourth to fifth year when it will settle into a natural approach to church life – both gathered and scattered.

This is why it takes patient urgency. It needs people willing to keep banging the drum for whole-life disciple-making longer and with more determination than they might have expected.

The way to sustain the changes is to revisit continually the foundations of whole-life discipleship. You must ensure that the vision of the Lordship of Christ over the universe and the church is presented continuously, so that people never unwittingly retreat to a personalized therapeutic form of Christianity. The focus of the church's prayer and ministry needs to continue to take into consideration the places where people already are. This needs to bring the challenge to see what God is doing in and through those contexts. Changes that will enhance the call to whole-life discipleship need to keep on being introduced.

The challenge of spiritual resistance

There is one aspect of the Christian life that has been assumed throughout this discussion, rather than being explicitly named. That central practice is prayer. If whole-life disciple-making communities are as important as we have suggested – if they are the means of unlocking the missionary force of God's people, if they are the places from where the good news of God is incarnated – then we need to recognize that we will enter into a spiritual conflict.

As Christians, we believe that a desire to release the people of God to serve him well will attract the attention of the enemy. On the whole, it would seem reasonable to suppose that the enemy cares little about what happens in churches as long as it remains private. Os Guinness's warning about our activities being privately engaging but publicly irrelevant would seem to be the perfect solution to the enemy of God's people.[1]

So before we charge off into the sunset, there's a moment to recognize that this process may come with a cost attached. In response to such opposition, first, we remember that Paul's clear guidance to disciples is that in the midst of this struggle we 'pray in the Spirit on all occasions with all kinds of prayers and requests . . . always keep on praying for all the saints' (Ephesians 6:18).

Ultimately, it is this reminder to pray that will save the process of change from being mechanistic, or indeed, manipulative. We need to keep on reminding ourselves that it's God who is at work among us; that we are cooperating with his desires.

Secondly, in the face of opposition, we remember that there is something worth struggling for here: the freedom of the people of God to live for his purposes, wherever they are, and to see the fruitfulness promised by Jesus to his disciples:

> Very truly I tell you, whoever believes in me will do the works I have been doing, and they will do even greater things than these, because I am going to the Father. And I will do whatever you ask in my name, so that the Father may be glorified in the Son. You may ask me for anything in my name, and I will do it. (John 14:12–14)

You'd be wise to think through whether you're willing to pay that price before you really begin.

Why you don't need to wait

If you're a leader, you don't have to wait. You can include this whole-life perspective the very next time you preach. You may be in the middle of a sermon series, or following a lectionary; it matters little. Once you begin to see what God's purposes are for the whole of his creation, and you see how he will take our everyday lives to make a difference, you will begin to see Scripture differently each time you engage with it.

- You do not need to begin a series on 'work'; you just need to recognize that many of your listeners do work.
- You do not need to present a whole new vision for the church that will take years to be adopted; you simply have to ask people what is happening in the places where they spend most of their time, who is there and what they think God might be doing.
- You do not need to stop pastoral visits, but you can engage in them with a wider purpose, recognizing that you are self-consciously trying to encourage people to grow as disciples.
- You do not need to spend lots of time explaining why you have changed; you could just invite people to come to a workshop to explore what would help them live more fruitfully for Christ.
- You can start today.

And once you do start, you will find it difficult to stop. It will become second nature.

If you're not a leader, you don't have to wait. You may feel that you have little formal authority in the church, but you can begin new conversations with people.

- You can promise to pray for the situations that people are facing in their everyday lives as they crop up in conversation and then, importantly, go back within a couple of weeks to ask them what happened.
- You can let your church leader know what challenges and opportunities you are facing and ask them to pray for you. And then, importantly, let them know what happened!
- You can pray that your church will change. If that feels too simple, you are underestimating the significance of prayer. If you think it won't change anything, you need to ask yourself whether you think God has finished with your particular congregation.
- You can encourage people to investigate the message of whole-life discipleship by reading the various publications from LICC or watching the original *Imagine* DVD.

You can be at the birth of a revolution in your own church.

How will you know you have changed?

There's a danger at this point of painting a utopian picture. We can end up suggesting some sort of perfectionism which is not only unrealistic, but also an unbiblical expectation. However, there should be fruit of the changes that have been introduced. The challenge will be that most of the institutional benchmarks of 'success' may not be relevant. We will not be able to measure fruitfulness by ABC (Attendance – how many people come on Sundays; Buildings – what is their condition; and Cash – how much do we have in the bank?) alone, but also on 'D' – disciples. How are we doing at helping people grow as whole-life disciples?

It also has to be remembered that the goal of all this envisioning, listening and changing is not that we have a more fulfilling, or even more relevant, experience of church together. The purpose is that people might play their part in God's mission in the world and live fruitful lives when they are scattered throughout towns and cities in their everyday lives. It is important that this fruitfulness is recognized and celebrated.

So where can you look to see whether people have grasped the implications of a renewed relationship between the church in its gathered state and in its scattered life?

Here are some suggestions.

Leaders will have changed when . . .

1. They have a concern not only for the general health of their congregation, but will be constantly asking pertinent questions about how congregational life is enabling the development of disciples of Jesus. They will not waste the opportunities for growth that come their way. So, for example, if there are unsettling situations happening in the church, the leaders will not want merely to smooth things over, but will be actively seeking a way for these to become growth moments for everyone. During the time we were working alongside one church, they had to deal with someone who was encouraging a group of people to leave and set up a church somewhere else. A tricky and painful situation. The challenge for the leaders was not to keep the situation quiet, nor to think of these people as the enemy, but to help the whole church understand what forgiveness, mediation and peacemaking looked like in practice, so that they might learn and apply it for

themselves in personal situations, should the need arise. If you want to disciple people in the ways of Jesus, you can't afford to waste these difficult opportunities when they arise.

2. They constantly want to learn more about the situations that people are facing in their everyday lives. They will also ensure that the overall ministry of the church takes these opportunities and challenges into account. For example, leaders might be visiting people more often to understand what was happening, and would be explicitly taking these circumstances into account when making future plans.

3. They recognize and live with the tension of wanting to recruit people for church activities and programmes, and yet coming to terms with the reality that people may have other demands on their lives that they need to honour. It's this tension that will be evidence of a change from an overemphasis on the gathered church at the expense of everything else. So, though it's an obvious point, if there are a number of teachers in the congregation, it makes sense to take into account the rhythm of the school year so that congregational activities are helpful, rather than another pressure in a difficult period.

4. They automatically reflect on how their preaching and worship leading will be relevant to a range of situations in their congregation's lives.

5. They see that their primary identity is not as a disciple-maker, but as a disciple. Therefore they will recognize that their own work setting (the church) is their frontline, having the potential to shape them into Christ-likeness or into hollow bitterness. They will see that this is where they are being formed as a disciple.

A congregation will have changed when . . .

1. Conversations begin to change. Alongside the necessary and enjoyable small talk, relationships will be developing that will sustain people as disciples in the rough and tumble of life. The expectation of people in the congregation will be that each of them has a vital role in helping one another grow as whole-life disciples. They will see that the seemingly small conversations and encouragements are not about being nice to each other, but are crucial ongoing reminders that we are called to make a difference where we are.

2. People recognize that the activities of the church are designed to help them see the wonder of God, give them a wider perspective on the world and provide a sharper insight into the way God is at work in that world through his people. They will be able to discern how the pattern of their life together works towards these aims.

3. They regularly hear the stories of ordinary lives lived for God's glory, seeing this dignifying of people's stories as vital redeeming work. This telling of stories liberates people to see their own lives differently, encouraging others to be equally creative. This will include the reality that life gets complicated at times through experiences of doubt, depression, grief and illness. However, these situations will be seen to be opportunities where genuine growth as disciples is possible, rather than unfortunate incidents that need to be dealt with quickly.

4. People begin to know one another's whole lives better and are prepared to be more supportive to one another in their overall context and in the particular missional context of their frontline.

5. Christians who join the church from another congregation will be able to recognize that they have come into a place with a very different culture.

Individual Christians will have changed when . . .

1. They have embraced their everyday contexts in such a way that they can believe that God could use them there for his purposes.
2. Their prayers are less defensive ('Lord, help me get through the day') and more desirous of discerning what God might do ('Lord, help me to understand what is happening so that I can live for your glory').
3. They have a renewed understanding about why their everyday frontlines (wherever they are and however many they are) matter to God, and when they are more able to be content with their situation, recognizing that they are not where they are by mere accident.
4. They are aware of the ongoing call to be a disciple of Jesus – a continuous lifestyle of allowing their characters and actions to be shaped by a profound understanding of Jesus and the demands of the kingdom. This will be fed and sustained by a growth in wisdom, which will be shaped through prayer and grappling with Scripture. They will be aware of the call to change.
5. Ultimately, there will be fruit that matches the question from earlier – 'How will the UK be reached?' Therefore, people will begin to have experience not only of living out their faith with integrity, but also of seeing other people intrigued by their way of life, wanting to know the reason for the hope that they have. People will become used to seeing others come to faith through their life of bearing witness to the Lordship of Christ.

The determination of the faithful

Of course, we remain flawed, attracted by good intentions that sometimes never translate into different actions. However, we are also people who are in transition. The existing culture of the churches that many are living with has not produced whole-life disciples. There needs to be a change – and that change has to be more than a revamped model of the old practices. We need a new disciple-making culture that is firmly missional and firmly located in our everyday world.

The process of change that has been laid out here is straightforward. There is nothing here that is difficult to grasp, nothing particularly contentious. We do not need anything more complicated. The church is called to be a gathering of God's people, liberated by the salvation offered through the work of Jesus, led by the Spirit of God who breathes his life into the people of God. The actions we have suggested are simple ones, and should take into account the journey that a church has been on, the style of that particular church and its tradition, and the aspirations of the members.

The potency of the process lies in the reality that it's the culture of the church which needs to change. As we have said, another programme bolted on to the existing range of activities will not be enough. Something more fundamental needs to take place. Cultures are notoriously difficult to change, but they can change and they do change. The statement 'Nothing will ever change here' is always the mark of a toxic despair. Things can change.

However, it will take determination, persistence and mutual encouragement. It may take years of sowing, listening and small changes before you can see all the fruits you would hope to see. But those willing to be faithful in following a vision of what is possible, willing to look for the green shoots of growth and willing to be persistent in believing that God has not given up on us all, will be rewarded for their years of patience.

The stakes are high and are worth fighting for.

- The people of God can be freed to know that there is no sacred–secular divide that excludes much of their lives from God's purpose.
- The church can be freed to live as a community, called to bring God's glory, knowing that members need one another's support in order to discern what God is doing in, around and through them.
- The leaders of churches can be freed from feeling that they are merely keeping an institution propped up, to knowing that they have a ministry of equipping that will make a difference to many people.
- Those who are unaware of God's love for them can be freed to gain a new insight into the whole-life significance of the life and teaching of Jesus.

Surely this is significant enough. And is worth the time and effort that is needed to renegotiate the gathered-scattered church relationship. It's worth the time and effort in seeing how Sunday can make all the difference to Monday. It's worth the time to ensure that all of us grow in our understanding of what it means to say 'Jesus is Lord' and live our everyday lives on the rock of that great truth.

It is hard to quantify how people have responded but I see a growing awareness that we can't compartmentalize our lives and it is fun when we don't. I think we have a long way to go, but I do think we have a culture developing where we are

trying to connect Monday with Sunday. I think it is in the DNA. People don't notice it terribly, but it is just there. People are becoming more confident and they are recognizing that discipleship is supposed to be 24/7.
Church leader

Moving onwards – guidelines and resources

This section offers some resources for the journey:

1. The next steps: a reflection guide for leaders or church members
2. Fuel for the journey: key books and resources we've found helpful along the way
3. A reminder of the big picture: a summary of the process that can also be downloaded as a poster for your church

To learn more or join the conversation, find tools, resources and tips, new ideas and insights, receive updates or share lessons you are learning, check out the Imagine section of LICC's website at www.licc.org.uk/imagine or call 020 7399 9555.

If you want to be kept in touch about future events and training, email imagine@licc.org.uk.

The next steps: a reflection guide

1. Pause for thought

If you can, take a moment to consider what you have read and begin to think through your responses.

You may want to begin by starting to articulate how what has been outlined resonates with your experience.

- How does what you have read make you feel – does it seem exciting, overwhelming, impossible, a nice idea?
- Are there ways in which things you have felt before have been illuminated? Alternatively, what are the questions that remain for you?

In turn, you may want to think about your own discipleship.

- Identify the key moments in which you grew as a believer. Where were they? What was happening?

- Think through the places where you are in an ordinary week and consider how God may think about your interactions in those places and your purposes in them.
- Is it possible that God has a compelling reason for you being in these places?
- Thinking about what the term 'whole-life disciple' means to you, do you feel equipped to make a difference in the places where you spend most of your time?

On a wider level, you might want to begin to think about your church and the people who are members there, whether you are a leader or not.

- What can you affirm that is happening there that supports people to grow as whole-life disciples?
- Can you see how this vision might become a reality in your context?

2. What you could do in the next two weeks

If you're a leader . . .

- You could talk to one other person about what struck you as you read through this book. This will begin to highlight the issues that are most important to you.
- You could look through your diary and think through the emphasis of your ministry: with which people do you spend most time? What are the topics of conversation? What are you not talking about? Why? How could you change that?
- You could make an appointment to meet three or four people in order to listen to the challenges and

opportunities they face in their everyday lives. You must determine to go in order to learn and resist the temptation to give advice.

- You could think through the sermons you have preached in the past six months. To what extent have they focused on the concerns or mission of the gathered church, or the pastoral concerns that people are facing, and to what extent have they been intentionally enabling people to grow as disciples? Have they had the desired effect? How do you know?

- If you are persuaded by the call to grow as a whole-life missionary disciple-making church, you could think about how you could share this message with your church leaders.

Some resources to get started

The Imagine Pilot Project grew out of the inspiration of Mark Greene's illustrated essay, *Imagine: How We Can Reach the UK*. It's short and easy to read, and it clarifies the missional challenge and why disciple-making is so central to meeting it. A fifty-minute *Imagine* vision-casting DVD was also produced with accompanying guidelines for groups.

A more recent essay that highlights the challenge of the sacred–secular divide is *The Great Divide* by Mark Greene. It takes on one of the most powerful 'enemies' of whole-life discipleship and helps us to see how dualistic thinking manifests itself in so many areas of life.

If you're not a leader . . .

- Think about how a renewed vision of the Lordship of Christ would have a transforming effect on the way you see the whole of your life.

- Reflect on how you have grown as a disciple and what caused the greatest changes in your understanding of what it means to be a Christian.
- Write down what your frontline is, noting who is there, what is happening and then discerning what you need prayer for.
- Talk to one other person about what you have read and thought, and why it is has been significant for you.
- Talk to your church leader about what you have been thinking and why you feel it would be good news for the church of which you are a part.

3. What could you do in the next two months

If you're a leader . . .

- Encourage your fellow leaders in the church to read this book and set up a relaxed discussion time together.
- Decide that the preaching ministry of the church would explicitly concentrate on exploring the implications of the Lordship of Christ.
- Reflect on the extent to which the pastoral care contract has been unwittingly accepted by the whole church and come to some decisions about how you could widen the contract to pastoral equipping in your own work and that of small group leaders, and/or pastoral visitors.
- Share the vision with a few people who could become a core team who will champion the whole-life cause.
- Decide whether the church could use the survey to discover the activities that have helped people grow as whole-life disciples and what could be done together to encourage further growth.

- Meet a number of members of the church congregation to learn more about their challenges and opportunities.
- Talk with someone from LICC about the spiritual and emotional cost that might be involved in your situation if you decide to take up the challenge to become a whole-life disciple-making church. If this is helpful, you might want to ask that person to keep you accountable to the decisions you will take.
- Talk with other church leaders in your locality about this. You could become a cluster-group of whole-life disciple-making churches.

If you're not a leader . . .

- You could have some intentional conversations with people in your church about the challenges and opportunities that they face in their everyday lives as disciples of Jesus.
- Depending on the response of the leadership to your earlier conversation, you could offer to be part of a small team of champions for this in your own church.
- You could ask someone to pray for, or with, you on a regular basis that you will live a consistent Christian life on your frontlines.
- You could take intentional steps to being a sign of God's blessing to people around you – this might involve some acts of kindness that are unusual because of the surrounding culture and / or could mean that you are looking for the opportunities to have very honest and natural conversations about your faith.

Within a year, the church could be having very different kinds of conversations; people could be experiencing fruitfulness in their whole lives; Christians living missionally could be bringing those they meet on their frontlines to a new awareness of the claims of Christ on their lives.

Fuel for the journey: resources and links

In order to keep your vision clear and focused, you'll need to have ongoing encouragement. The books and resources below will offer this to you. In addition, you'll find updates on what we and others involved in the Imagine Project are learning on the Imagine website.

Resources for use by church members

Thinking about whole-life discipleship

Resources for personal study
Billington, Antony, Killingray, Margaret and Parry, Helen,
    Whole Life, Whole Bible (BRF, 2011).
This is a collection of fifty reflections that take a reader through the whole Bible narrative. Originally written as part of LICC's weekly 'Word for the Week', the reflections provide whole-life disciples with food for the journey, but also give them ideas to see how whole-life the whole Bible is.

Greene, Mark, *Imagine: How We Can Reach the UK* (LICC, 2003).
The original essay that identified whole-life discipleship as the missing element in church life.

Greene, Mark, *The Great Divide* (LICC, 2010).
Distributed at the Lausanne World Congress, 2010, this booklet addresses the problem of the sacred–secular divide head on.

Peterson, Eugene, *A Long Obedience in the Same Direction* (Inter-Varsity Press, 1980).
This has been reprinted so many times because this reflection on the Psalms of Ascent (120 – 134) is so vital for people desiring to grow as disciples.

Wright, Chris, *The Mission of God's People* (Zondervan, 2010).
A book exploring the truth that the mission of God will only make sense to people if they see something different. It challenges us to live differently because we are committed to God's mission.

Yuill, Chick, *Moving in the Right Circles* (Inter-Varsity Press, 2011).
For both individuals and groups, this explores what it means to live an authentic Christian life.

Small group resources
LICC, *Imagine* (DVD) (LICC, 2006).
This is a tried and tested resource that's good for raising the basic issues.

Practicing Our Faith: www.practicingourfaith.org

Thinking about the frontline

Resources for personal study
Books that help people take seriously their ordinary lives as being the arena for God to be at work:

Hardyman, Julian, *Maximum Life* (Inter-Varsity Press, 2009).
Kandiah, Krish, *Twenty-four: Integrating Faith and Real Life* (Authentic, 2007).
Stackhouse, Ian, *This Day Is Yours* (Paternoster, 2008).

Small group resources
Keller, Tim, *Gospel in Life* (Zondervan, 2010).

LICC, *Imagine: Life on the Frontline* (LICC, 2011).
This is designed to help small groups understand, support and disciple one another through their experiences of their frontlines.

EA, Square Mile (www.eauk.org/squaremile/life-discipleship-equipping.cfm).

Thinking about the frontline of work

Resources for personal study
Books that help people in work think through the challenges and opportunities they have there to thrive and be fruitful disciples:

Coffey, Ian, *Working It Out: God, You and the Work You Do* (Inter-Varsity Press, 2008).
Greene, Mark, *Thank God It's Monday* (rev. ed.) (SU, 2001).
Parmiter, John, *Ten at Work* (Inter-Varsity Press, 2011).

Valler, Paul, *Get a Life: Winning Choices for Working People* (Inter-Varsity Press, 2008).

Wynne, Jago, *Working Without Wilting* (Inter-Varsity Press, 2009).

Small group resources

LICC, *Christian Life and Work* (LBC Productions, 2000).

A reminder of the big picture

Throughout the book we've emphasized that the necessary changes are long-term ones. So there need to be reminders that this is not this month's special emphasis, but is the long-term direction that a church is going to take. Mark Greene has produced a poster reflecting the process and values of the whole-life journey that could be used to remind a congregation what they are involved in, and this has been reproduced below. It can also be downloaded from LICC's website, where all the asterisked references will become clear.

---

1. Release the vision . . . root it in the whole-life Gospel
– it's Jesus-following, it's cross-shaped, it's Spirit-empowered, it's central, it's missional, it's liberating. It's for everyone and it needs everyone: cleaners and accountants, builders and barristers, 7 year olds and 77 year olds. It's for out there as well as in here, it's for others as well as us, it takes a long time and it's hard. It's a revolution, it's the way things are meant to be and it's urgent . . .

---

2. Focus on fruitfulness – this isn't about making the church run more smoothly but helping God's people be more fruitful in all of life – M & M & M & M & . . . * modelling godliness, ministering grace, making culture anew, being a mouthpiece for the Gospel . . .

3. Find and empower the championing team – the SWAT team who really, really want to make this happen. Make sure there are lay and church-paid members . . .

4. Create a new community conversation – help each other express it and imagine its implications and challenges together – use the DVD,* the questionnaires,* small group materials,* prayer meetings, special meetings, fridge magnets, whatever gets everyone talking to everyone . . .

5. Start small but strategic – let the yeast get to work, help the whole church identify and introduce mustard seeds, Trojan mice, one-degree shifts* that carry the new DNA . . .

6. Learn to see everything through the frontline lens – this is a process not a programme, so everything may not change but the way and the why you do everything probably will, from the coffee rota* to the sermon,* make sure the yeast gets kneaded into every cranny of church life . . .

7. Celebrate progress, tell the stories – frontline testimonies – FTs. No FT, no progress. You'll know you're succeeding when people tell the stories of what's going on out there: at the school gate, in the supermarket, the office, the club. Invite the stories and make sure they are told in a way that connects clearly to whole-life principles. These are stories about God at work – wonderful fuel for praise in prayer and worship . . .

8. Cultivate a biblical imagination – teach, preach, pray, chat with the aim of developing a gospel-shaped, whole-life, Spirit-filled, biblical imagination . . .

9. Expand the pastor/people contract – from PC world* – pastoral care – to dynamic all-church pastoral care/pastoral equipping for all of life. This isn't just about the 'leader' adding pastoral equipping to their role; it's about the whole community recognizing the kind of people that the pastor is there to help you become and the kind of people you are there to help one another become . . .

10. Walk the talk – and remember this walk is costly. It's often uncomfortable learning to do new things and it's uncomfortable being God's person out in some pretty difficult places. It's a cross we're taking up, not a hobby. Work out how the pastor and the paid team need to change their week to understand the frontlines the people are on, and to identify the skills and perspectives and prayer the people on the frontline need, and the skills and perspectives and prayer the leaders need . . .

11. Love one another. Crawl, stumble, walk in grace and in step with the Spirit – whole-life discipleship is not intended to be the latest new salvation by works, a whole set of hurdles to jump, a whole new way to feel inadequate and guilty. So cheer one another on. You're all learning to change – and God is your gracious Father, not a finger-wagging, grumpy old headmaster. This is a lifelong journey – a long walk in a new direction, not a sprint to be completed by next September . . .

12. Never surrender – the leisure time/neighbourhood Christianity default setting is very strong. Fight for the whole-life Gospel life in prayer, fight for it in Bible study, fight for it in song choice, fight for it in home groups, fight for it in bulletins and announcements and web communications, fight for it in business meetings and training programmes and budget allocation: never surrender.

* = find out more on the LICC website: www.licc.org.uk/imagine

I am sometimes asked what is happening with the Imagine Project, often in a tone that gently suggests that the answer might be, 'Not much', since it doesn't seem to have a very high profile. But the low profile is intentional: I have purposefully not 'badged' most of our activities as Imagine Project activities. One day, the project will come to an end, but my dream is that – by then – the values that it is seeking to promote will have worked their way so deeply into our DNA that we will be living them out without the need for a project title to remind us what we are about.

Member and leader of Champions Team,
Imagine Pilot Church

Notes

Beginnings and the bigger picture

1. M. Greene, 'Mission World: One More Wall To Go', *EG*, March 2011 (LICC), www.licc.org.uk.

Chapter 4: How to become a whole-life disciple-making church

1. See 'Fuel for the journey' at the end of this book, and visit www.licc.org.uk for more resources.
2. A copy of the survey along with directions about how to get the best out of it can be downloaded from www.licc.org.uk/imagine.
3. For more details, see Mark Greene's article, 'TTT Time', in *EG*, September 2009. You can read this online at www.licc.org.uk, by searching for the title.
4. These questions have been used by a church in the USA whose minister has been following the principles of whole-life discipleship for many years: www.ucc.org/assets/pdfs/crabtree.pdf.

Chapter 5: All learning together

1. M. Gibbs, 'No More Spiritual Babies: The Development of a Strong Laity', keynote address to Lutheran Church LAOS Theologians' Colloquium, 23 May 1982, accessed at www.vesper.org.
2. S. Simmel, 'Why Would Laypeople Want Theological Education, Anyway?', accessed at www.alban.org/conversation.aspx?id=8798.

Chapter 7: As you begin . . .

1. O. Guinness, *The Last Christian on Earth* (Regal, 2010), p. 80.